200 Beading Tips, Techniques & Trade Secrets

200 Beading Tips, Techniques & Trade Secrets

Jean Power

St. Martin's Griffin
New York

Library of Congress Cataloging-in-
Publication Data available upon request.

ISBN-10: 0-312-58747-3
ISBN-13: 978-0-312-58747-5

QUAR.BTTT

First published in the United States by
St. Martin's Press

Conceived, designed, and produced by
Quarto Publishing plc
The Old Brewery
6 Blundell Street
London N7 9BH

Project editor: Chloe Todd Fordham
Art editor: Jacqueline Palmer
Designer: Paul Griffin
Illustrator: Kuo Kang Chen
Photographer: Martin Norris
Copy editor: Ruth Patrick
Proofreader: Céline Hughes

Art director: Caroline Guest
Creative director: Moira Clinch
Publisher: Paul Carslake

Color reproduction by
PICA Digital Pte Ltd, Singapore
Printed in China by
1010 Printing International

First U.S. Edition: October 2009

10 9 8 7 6 5 4 3 2 1

Contents

Introduction

Beading and jewelry making are talents and interests which have woven their way through different ages and cultures. Learning to make and perfect your own jewelry is a skill that not only brings you pleasure while you engage in it, but can also give you the joy of having a new piece of jewelry—or other ornamentation—as the end result.

If you have ever been interested in learning how to bead, string, or use wire, then this book will give you all the necessary techniques and know-how to get started. If you are more experienced, then read on to learn all those tips, fix-its, and trade secrets to ensure your work is finished to the highest quality.

About this book

The information in this book is organized by technique and divided into four chapters:

Getting started (pages 9–45):
This chapter presents an overview on jewelry-making basics, from selecting your beads and equipment to essential design choices

Stringing (pages 47–67):
From threading your needle to experimenting with creative knotwork and finishes, you will find all you need to know about this popular technique inside these pages.

Wirework (pages 69–85):
Cut, manipulate, and file your wire; turn loops; fashion charms; and create decorative coils—the possibilities are endless in the world of wirework.

Beadweaving (pages 87–149):
Working with seed beads requires patience and skill: step-by-step photography will guide you through the principle beading stitches, teach you to follow patterns and charts, and inspire you to get beading right away!

Beading tips:
Hundreds of numbered tips outline insider secrets and professional advice that will enable beaders of every level to achieve excellent results.

"Try it" panels:
These panels contain great ideas for experimenting with methods and beading materials, and will inspire you to develop your own projects and preferred beading techniques.

Step-by-step sequences:
Full-color photography teaches you new techniques in easy-to-follow step-by-step sequences. Any difficult turns or stitches are reiterated in a detailed close-up, to help you achieve professional results.

Finished examples:
Jewelry samples show you what you can achieve with new-learned techniques, and will inspire you to begin projects of your own.

"Fix it" panels:
These regular companion features contain useful advice on how to avoid or correct a mistake in your beadwork.

See also:
This panel refers you to other related articles in the book.

Fold-out flap
This useful pull-out page, which you will find at the back of the book, can be folded out while the book is open. Size-up your seed beads as you work, and estimate bead quantities using this handy feature.

Getting started

Jewelry making is a wonderful world filled with beads, color, design, and fun! Whether you choose stringing, wirework, beadweaving, or a combination of all three styles, there are many general tips and techniques that will make your life easier as well as give you the knowledge to make the right choices.

SEE ALSO:

Jewelry-making tools,
page 22
Designing with color,
page 32

Beginning with beads

Beads fall into two main categories: natural or man-made. Within each category there are various types of beads, each of which have their own qualities and characteristics. The choices you make will depend on different factors: your preferences for color and shape; the intended recipient; your budget; the look you have in mind; and what's available to you. However, always remember the main motivation for buying beads—you must like the look of them.

1 Man-made beads

Man-made beads can be made of glass, crystal, fake pearl, polymer clay, and many other materials.

GLASS BEADS

The most common and easy-to-find beads are those made of glass. They're made all over the world, using many different techniques and are available in just about every size, shape, and color you could want. You can buy them individually, on strands, by weight, or by count.

Lampwork beads

A separate category of glass beads are lampwork beads. These are handmade and are often one-of-a-kind, or small editions. Their higher price reflects the time and care taken in making them and they can be used to add a special touch to any jewelry.

Some lampwork beads are now available with metal cores—these don't wear down as much as glass does when used on a thick metal chain.

Donut beads have large central holes.

Polymer clay beads often have fun, modern design patterns.

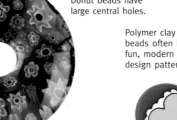

FIX IT

2 Beware of inferior lampwork

Glass beads are fragile when first made—they can crack and break very easily. To add strength, they should be annealed, which involves heating and then cooling them in a kiln. However, cheap lampwork beads made in the hundreds and thousands are not usually annealed, and that bag of lovely, colorful, cheap beads you bought can soon turn into a collection of useless half-beads. Always check with the seller that the beads you are interested in have been annealed.

3 Bead variations

Expand your definition of "bead" and you might be surprised at what you come up with. If it has a hole you can string thread through, then you can use it as a bead. Try washers, pasta shapes, sequins, buttons, and much more.

CRYSTALS

Crystals are a category of glass bead. Prices for crystals vary dependent on many factors:

• Workmanship
Austrian crystals are the most expensive. For a more affordable option, choose crystals made in countries like the Czech Republic, or use fire-polished beads. These are either molded or cut, and then heated at a high temperature to give them a glossy surface and shine.

• Sharpness
The sharpness of the surface facets will affect the crystal's value. Those with sharper, more plentiful facets have the most sparkle and dazzle.

• Shape
Some shapes are harder to cut so carry a premium. Any shaping or adding of facets increases the likelihood of wasted stone, so remember: When you buy these facets, you are also paying for those that had to be thrown away.

PEARLS

Eternally popular, and no longer just for your grandmother's single strand, pearls are now widely available and affordable. Check you know what you're buying as it's not always easy to tell the real thing from glass or plastic.

Identifying real and fake pearls

A strand of real pearls will never contain identical-looking beads. There will be slight variations in colors, shapes, and sizes that won't appear in fake pearls. Furthermore, the surface of a real pearl won't be as smooth as that of a fake one. You may be able to identify this by sight and touch, or even by rubbing it on the surface of your teeth!

If the outer coating peels away, the pearl may be fake.

Real pearls will have irregular surface features.

4 Natural beads

This is a wide category which includes pearls and semi-precious beads, but is commonly used to describe beads made of wood, shell, seeds, bone, or stone. Natural beads are available in a wide range of sizes, shapes, and finishes. You can buy unfinished wooden beads, simply varnished, or fully decorated. You can combine natural beads with suitable materials for a more earthy or ethnic look, or contrast with metals and colors for a contemporary look.

Natural beads can be bought in their natural colors or dyed depending on the look you want.

Choose fire-polished beads for an affordable option.

While sharp facets give you the sparkle you're after, they can also cut your stringing material, so be sure to choose what you use carefully.

SEMI-PRECIOUS

Also known as gemstones, semi-precious are those more affordable, natural, mined stones. These are commonly available in many different shapes, cuts, colors, and sizes—from small chips to large chunks.

There's nothing wrong with using fake pearls if they give you the look you are after.

SEE ALSO:

Size and shape,
page 16
Jewelry-making tools,
page 22

Seed beads and more

Not all seed beads are the same. Once you start buying and using them, you'll soon see a difference in size, shape, and quality between country of origin, manufacturers, and even individual colors. All of these add up to making the difference between an even, professional finish and an uneven, more free-form one. While either result is great in context, you want to make sure you get the one you want.

Cylinder beads are regular in size and shape. Their flat sides mean they sit together closely and their even sizing will make your work neat and precise.

5 Seed beads

"Seed beads" is the name given to the smallest type of glass beads. These are generally under $\frac{1}{5}$ in (4mm) in size and shaped like a donut.

SIZES
Seed beads are sold by size, ranging from around size 22 and smaller, up to size 6, with the most common sizes being 15, 11, 8, and 6. As the bead size number increases, the physical size of each bead decreases. This is because the numbers are based on the "aught" sizing system, which originally specified how many beads fitted into a given bead. So a size 15 is a lot smaller than a size 6. You can buy seed beads individually, on strands, by weight, or by count.

6 Cylinder beads

Cylinder beads are a variant of seed beads, as they are small in size, but their shape is very different. They are cylinder-shaped with flat sides that fit closely together, giving your work a neat, regular look. This is achieved by the accuracy with which these beads are made. The main size they are available in is 11, but you can now buy them in smaller sizes, as well as the popular "double" size, which is not only double the width of a regular cylinder bead, but also double the length. Whatever the size, these beads have large holes, which not only makes them ideal for stitches where you want to thread through them multiple times, but also increases the amount you get as they weigh less.

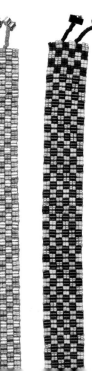

Double cylinder beads mix well with regular-sized cylinder beads.

The most common seed bead sizes are 15, 11, 8, and 6. They are shown here in various colors in ascending size order from top (15) to bottom (6).

FIX IT

7 Uneven beads?

To get a more even-sized, shaped, and holed bead, choose beads made in Japan over those made in the Czech Republic. You'll find that Japanese seed beads usually have larger holes, meaning that you can pass through them more times.

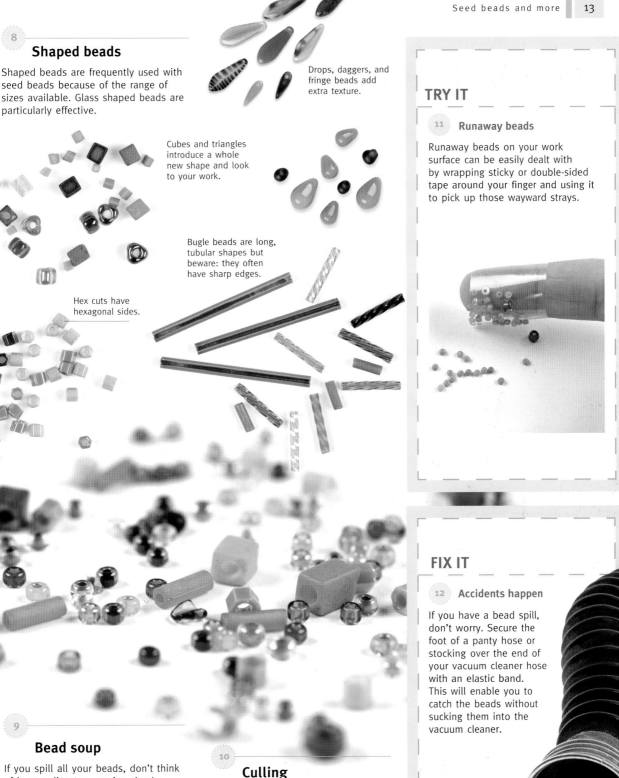

8 Shaped beads

Shaped beads are frequently used with seed beads because of the range of sizes available. Glass shaped beads are particularly effective.

Drops, daggers, and fringe beads add extra texture.

Cubes and triangles introduce a whole new shape and look to your work.

Bugle beads are long, tubular shapes but beware: they often have sharp edges.

Hex cuts have hexagonal sides.

9 Bead soup

If you spill all your beads, don't think of it as a disaster—you've simply made bead soup. You can sort your beads back into their separate categories if you prefer, but you can also keep the mix for a future project.

10 Culling

As you work, it's best to get rid of any beads that are misshapen or odd-sized. This will give a much better look to your finished work.

TRY IT

11 Runaway beads

Runaway beads on your work surface can be easily dealt with by wrapping sticky or double-sided tape around your finger and using it to pick up those wayward strays.

FIX IT

12 Accidents happen

If you have a bead spill, don't worry. Secure the foot of a panty hose or stocking over the end of your vacuum cleaner hose with an elastic band. This will enable you to catch the beads without sucking them into the vacuum cleaner.

Vintage beads

Definitions of "antique" vary from anything older than 100 years, made before 1900, or made before 1840—but when it comes to vintage, the definitions are even more varied.

Check metal beads to ensure no metal plating has peeled off.

SEE ALSO:

Jewelry-making tools, page 22
Designing with color, page 32

If what looks like metal feels lightweight, it may be plastic.

13

How "vintage" is vintage?

Some sellers define vintage as anything over twenty-five years old but under 100, so anything made right up to and including the start of the 1980s can qualify. But some sellers are less scrupulous and for them vintage can mean anything made up until yesterday! You can also come across the term "vintage style" for something made recently that looks old—it can get very confusing.

Check all faceted beads to ensure there is no damage.

Remember: what looks like cheap plastic may actually be Bakelite and quite valuable.

FIX IT

14   Recycling beads

Many strands of plastic beads are formed around the stringing thread—simply put, there are no real holes. Cutting these up to rework a design will leave you with lots of beads with string stuck in the center. A bead reamer (shown below) comes with different-sized files and enables you to make or enlarge a hole for stringing by smoothing any sharp edges.

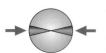

DRILLING YOUR BEADS
When drilled, beads can easily chip, so use the smallest drill you can find. If drilled all the way through, a bead can chip as the drill exits. To prevent this, drill from one side and then from another. This is a tricky technique as often the holes don't align or neither drill goes deep enough to leave a smooth hole.

15

Identifying vintage beads

When buying vintage or second-hand beads, it can be hard to know exactly what you're buying. The first rule is to examine them closely. Do this by sight, feel, and weight.

• **Sight:** Is there an obvious seam? If so, the beads may be molded plastic or pressed glass. If you're not convinced that what you're buying is what it says it is, use the taste test—do you like the look of them regardless of whether they're real or not? Buy them for their look and you'll be happy even if they don't turn out to be the bargain rubies you hoped you'd found.

• **Feel and weight:** If the beads are warm to the touch, don't make a clinking sound when knocked against each other, and are lightweight, you know they're more likely plastic. Glass would feel heavier, make a noise, and is colder when first held. The same rules apply when you are looking at gemstones or pearls.

Crystals are the most likely to chip, so always check them carefully.

This necklace could be broken down and used in lots of other projects; the pearls in one, the glass beads in another.

Treasure or trash

Beads and jewelry can be vintage or old, destined for the bin, or just in need of tender loving care. Before you buy something just because it's a bargain, examine it closely and work out if it really is good value for money.

Are the beads salvageable? Look for cracks, chips, or flaws which will stop you using them.

Are they real beads? If they're formed around the string they're on, you may not be able to use them in the way you intend. However, if you've got the patience, a bead reamer may help you to turn strands of beads into individual pieces (see opposite).

Do you like them? If you're buying them just because they're a bargain, you may find they'll sit unused in your bead box and you could have used the money for something you really like instead.

Even if the jewelry is damaged, you may find clasps or findings that are salvageable and worth buying for use in another piece.

Treasure jewelry

Odd beads, whether bought, found, discarded, or received as gifts, can be used to make jewelry that tells a story. Buy beads abroad on a special vacation and string them together to bring back memories of the trip. Or get together with beading friends, each choose a bead, then combine them to make a piece that will remind you of your friends.

Cloisonné beads may be a memento of a trip to China.

Throw out the rule book when creating treasure jewelry and mix beads regardless of color, size, type, or finish.

Size and shape

Beads are not just small and round! They come in all manner of sizes and shapes and these choices combine with those of color and material to give you an endless palette to play around with. The best way to learn which beads work together is to experiment to see what results you get and what effects you like. Geometric beads with sharp angles may seem hard and masculine to you, or modern and fun. Round beads may appear boring and basic, or classic and elegant. The choice is yours and learning what you like will make it easier for you to make choices and jewelry you're happy with.

SEE ALSO:

Planning your design, page 30
Fold-out flap, back of the book

Dagger beads add shape and texture.

Mixing different-shaped or different-sized beads in similar colors creates a united piece.

Even used in large quantities, seed beads can be used to add subtle detail to busy pieces.

Estimating quantities

You'll find that the size of beads varies according to manufacturer, finish on the bead, and even color of the bead. This table shows an approximation of the average sizes and quantities.

Bead (approximate size)	Beads per 1in (2.5cm)	Beads per 18in (46cm)	Beads per 24in (61cm)
Size 15 seed bead (1.5mm)	17	307	401
Size 11 seed bead (1.8–2.2mm)	12–14	210–256	278–339
Size 8 seed bead (3.3mm)	8	140	185
Size 6 seed bead (4mm)	6	115	153
2mm bead	12	230	305
3mm bead	8	154	203
4mm bead	6	115	153
5mm bead	5	92	122
6mm bead	4	77	102
8mm bead	3	57	76
10mm bead	2	46	61
12mm bead	2	38	51

The natural shape of these stones adds drama and surprise to this colorful bracelet.

Combine perfect shapes with imperfect ones and play with different textures.

19

Table of common seed beads

The table below shows the vital statistics of a number of common bead sizes. This will give you an idea of the physical size of each of the bead sizes and the amount of beads per gram.

	Seed bead size	Approximate size	Number per 1 gram	Number per 10 grams	Number per 100 grams
	Size 15	1.5 mm	250	2,500	25,000
	Size 11	2.2 mm	120	1,200	12,000
	Size 8	3 mm	36	360	3,600
	Size 6	3.7 mm	18	180	1,800
Cylinder bead size	Approximate size	Number per 1 gram	Number per 10 grams	Number per 100 grams	
Size 11	1.6 mm	200	2,000	20,000	

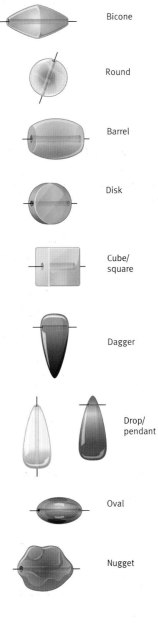

20

Common bead shapes

Not all beads are round. They come in many shapes and sizes. Below are some of the most common with their names and how their holes lie:

Bicone

Round

Barrel

Disk

Cube/ square

Dagger

Drop/ pendant

Oval

Nugget

Circles, squares, ovals, and drops play off each other to create a sense of cohesion.

he elegant hape of a drop ead is perfect r embellishing ne end of fringes r earrings.

Square silver beads work in tandem with circular coral ones in this bracelet.

Cords, threads, and memory wire

SEE ALSO:

Stringing tips and tricks, page 50
Crimping, page 52
Threads and knots, page 56
Using cord and ribbon, page 60
Using elastic, page 63
Using memory wire, page 64

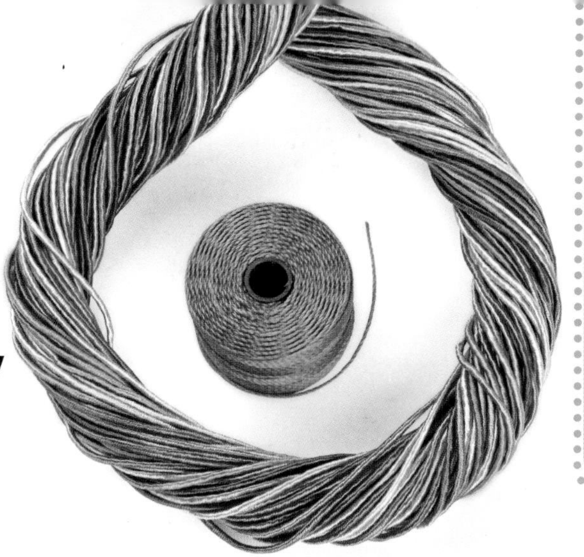

The world of beading is filled with different material choices. You can make your selection based on the technique you want to use, the look you're after, the ease of making a finished piece, or what's easily available to you.

21

Cord

Cord comes in many different materials, colors, and sizes. You will find satin, leather, cotton, or suede easily in shops. Satin cord is commonly sold as rattail and like other cords is widely available in widths of 1–2mm. Cord is ideal for knotting and you can choose to make it part of your design rather than hide it, so look for colors that complement or contrast with your beads (see page 33).

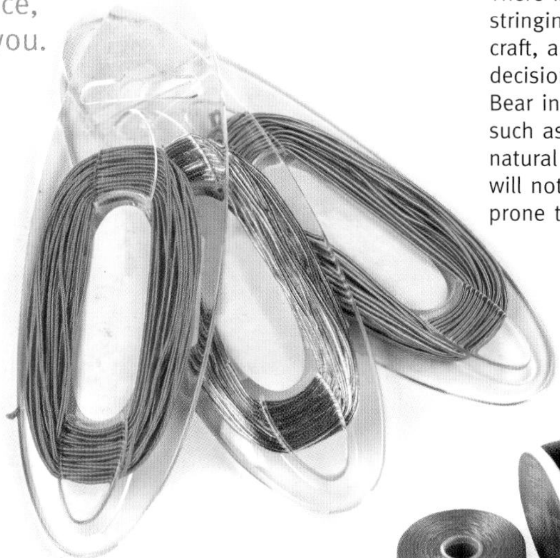

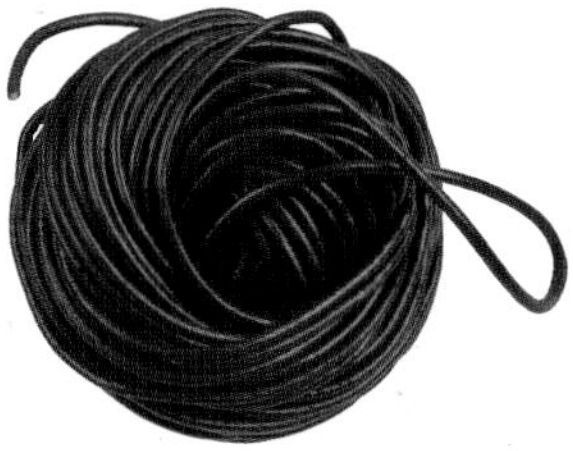

22

Thread

There is a wide range of suitable stringing thread available in jewelry, craft, and bead stores and the final decision on which one you use is yours. Bear in mind that a synthetic thread, such as nylon, will be tougher than a natural one, such as cotton or silk, and will not only last longer but is less prone to stretching.

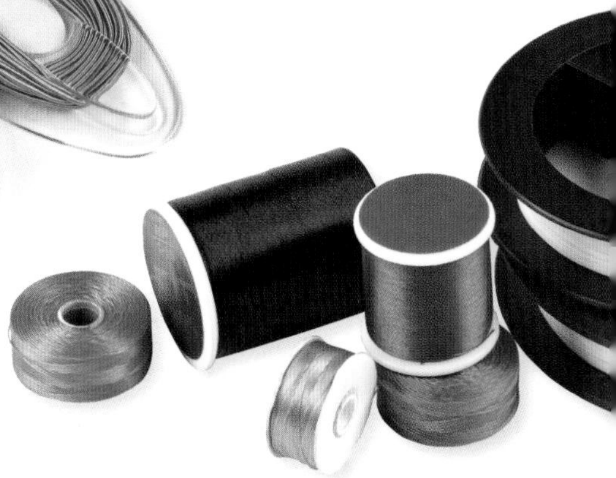

23

Ribbon

Whether they're made of fabric or metal yarn, ribbons can add a new texture and range of colors to any jewelry you make. Mesh and plastic ribbon is tube-shaped and is ideal for putting beads into as well as onto.

24

Illusion cord

Ideal for making illusion and floating necklaces, this fine cord comes in a variety of colors and can be easily knotted to keep beads in one place.

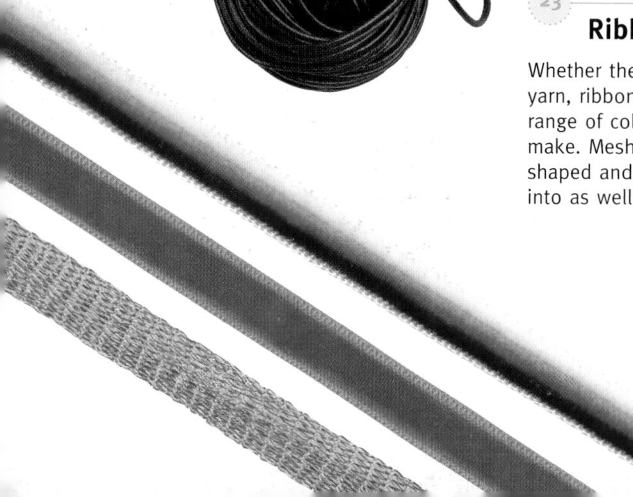

25

Beading elastic

Ideal for making children's jewelry or pieces for anyone who can't use clasps, beading elastic is available in a variety of thicknesses. The finer ones are harder to use, but you may find that the thicker ones won't go through all the holes in your beads.

26

Memory wire

Named because it holds its shape, memory wire is made of toughened steel and is available silver- or gold-plated. It can be bought in large reels or ready-cut pieces. It comes in bracelet, necklace, or ring sizes and is tough enough to take heavy or rough-holed beads. You need to ensure you use a special memory wire cutter because it will damage any others.

27

Flexible beading wire

Commonly used for crimping (see page 52), flexible beading wire is made of multiple fine strands of stainless steel coated with nylon. As it won't hold a knot, you need to add crimp beads, which are squashed to bite into the nylon and hold it securely. The more strands of steel—they are available in strands of 7, 19, and 49—the smoother a drape you'll find in your finished piece.

The nylon coating on flexible beading wire can wear away at the cut end, so it is important to make sure you cover the ends so that the steel strands don't cause injury to the wearer.

28

Gimp

Also called French wire, this useful material resembles a fine spring of metal. However, it does not have any spring to it and is easily damaged. Use it to cover your thread and protect it from wearing against metal findings.

FIX IT

29 Remove stretch

Ensure that you remove any stretch in your cords and threads before you finish the jewelry as they may stretch when worn and gaps will appear. To do this, thread your beads onto a long length of the material, tie the ends together, and leave to hang on a doorknob or coat hanger until needed. Even if you decide not to use that specific thread, you will still have a length of stretched material for another occasion.

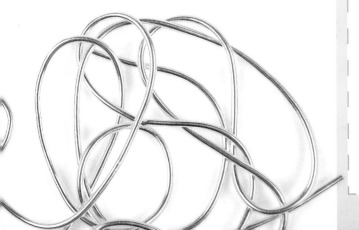

Working with wire

Wirework is all about the wire, but that's not as boring as it sounds. Wire is a versatile material available in a wide variety of metals, sizes, shapes, and colors—all of which will add a different look to your jewelry.

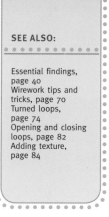

SEE ALSO:

Essential findings, page 40
Wirework tips and tricks, page 70
Turned loops, page 74
Opening and closing loops, page 82
Adding texture, page 84

Choosing metals

The most commonly used metal in wirework is sterling silver or silver-plated wire. Its popularity is due to its color, shine, ease of use, availability, and price. But don't feel limited to this. Choose the wire you want to use based on your preferences for the look as well as your budget.

PLATED AND COATED WIRES
Plated wires are a lot more affordable than those made completely of a more expensive metal. This makes them a more accessible option, but beware— some are cheaply made and you may find the coating coming off after a lot of handling or working. This may also occur if you decide to hammer your pieces, so experiment first to see if your choice will stand the test of time.

Plated metals don't have to be boring. Look out for colored metals to complement or contrast with your beads.

Gold-plated wire is a lot more affordable than the real thing.

COPPER
Copper is the perfect choice for experimenting with, for two reasons. Firstly, it is a lot more affordable than silver. Secondly, it is easy to tell copper apart from your silver wire so you won't mix them up, which is especially important if you're selling your work or saving scraps.

Silver wire is very popular and sterling silver is the brightest metal available.

Bronze is an unusual choice that could make your jewelry more unique.

Brass is a more affordable gold-colored metal.

31 Wire gauge

Wire is either sold in gauge (ga) or by millimeters (mm), both of which refer to its diameter. The gauge commonly used is American Wire Gauge (AWG). Although these don't match up exactly, a rough conversion is usually close enough for most wirework.

AWG	mm
38	0.1
34	0.15
32	0.2
30	0.25
28	0.3
26	0.4
24	0.5
22	0.6
21	0.7
20	0.8
19	0.9
18	1
16	1.2
14	1.5
12	2

32 Hard or soft?

Wire is sold in different levels of hardness: soft; hard; and half-hard, each of which has its ideal uses.

Hardness	Ideal for	Unsuitable for
Soft	Wrapping around another wire—it won't harden and become brittle as you work it.	Making clasps or components—it will be too soft to have the strength you need.
Hard	Making clasps and weight-bearing components—it has the strength to keep its shape.	Wrapping or any techniques that require a lot of work—the wire will become very difficult to manipulate and too hard on your hands.
Half-hard	All types of wirework—it is versatile. Don't choose half-hard if you need a really soft or hard wire, but otherwise it is an ideal substitute.	

33 Saving scraps

When working in wire, always save your scraps. These can be recycled and your metal merchant may purchase them from you for a store credit or more wire. Your scrap pot is also a great place to rummage through for a small piece of wire ideal to finish a project.

34 What size to use

The most commonly used size of wire is 20 ga (0.8mm). This is thick enough to have strength and fine enough not to be overpowering. It is also a comfortable size to fit through an ear piercing so is ideal when making earring findings (see page 40). If you're looking for something thicker, then 18 ga (1mm) or 16 ga (1.2mm) is perfect. If you want something finer then 32–26 ga (0.2–0.4mm) is great for wrapping and twisting.

20 ga (0.8mm) wire is the most useful size for jewelry making.

If you're looking for a thicker wire style then 18 ga (1mm) is a good choice.

32 ga (0.2mm) wire is a great size for wrapping around another wire.

SEE ALSO:

Pliers and wire cutters, page 26
Storage, page 28
Getting comfortable, page 44

Jewelry-making tools

There are lots of tools available in stores to assist you in your jewelry making. Read on to learn more about how each one can help you get the best finish.

An awl or large needle is ideal for moving knots.

35
Awl

This useful tool is essential if you want to ensure your knots end up where you want them, but equally you can use a large, blunt needle or even a toothpick or a cocktail stick. See page 56 for instructions on how to use your awl.

Choose the needle that feels best in your hand and fits through your beads.

36
Needles

Available in many sizes and thicknesses, the needle you choose when stringing or beadweaving is based on which fits through the beads you're using and which feels best in your hands. If you find your hand gets tired, try switching to a thicker needle.

Keep your needles safe in a container like this. It fits neatly in your beading kit and will keep the sharp points away from your work and hands.

37
Bead reamer

If the holes in your beads are small or they have sharp edges, this tool (with its specially designed files) is essential. Use it to carefully enlarge the holes in your beads. It is always best to do this under running water, partly because washing dust away from the file and hole will stop the bead from getting clogged up, partly because the fine dust produced when using a reamer (especially on some natural shells and beads) can be harmful—you want to ensure you don't breathe it in.

A reamer is perfect for enlarging or smoothing your bead holes.

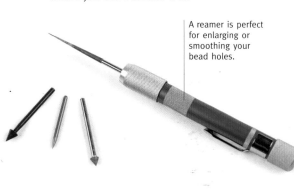

38
Bead design board

Planning your design before stringing becomes a lot easier with this specially designed board with its useful grooves and measurement indicators.

USING A BEAD DESIGN BOARD
Bead design boards are creative and practical spaces where you can experiment with the color, shape, size, and length of your beads before you string them all together into a final piece. Here's how it works:

The grooves:
The grooves on a design board are for you to place your beads in, and will help you to plan the individual strands of your finished piece. Experiment with color choices and the order of your beads here. Most bead design boards come with three grooves which enable you to plan a multistrand piece and see how the different strands will interact.

Measurements:
Around the outside and inside edges of the board are measurements to help you work out the exact length of your piece. When laying your beads on the board, make sure you don't leave any gaps as this will give you an inaccurate length.

Containers:
A bead design board has useful indentations that will hold beads and findings as you work.

Avoid losing beads by adding stoppers to the ends of your threads.

Prevent beads from rolling and getting lost by using a bead mat.

39 Bead Stoppers

Disaster can strike and when it does, you'll be glad you used these. Simply clip a Bead Stopper onto your stringing material and when you accidentally drop your work, you won't hear the sound of your beads spilling over the floor. If you don't have Bead Stoppers, a paperclip, knot, or even some tape can be used.

40 Bead tray/scoop

Bead scoops are perfect for getting your beads back from your working surface and into your tubes or bags.

Bead scoops are available in various shapes and sizes.

41 Bead mat

Although you can work on most surfaces, a specially designed bead mat will make life a lot easier. Not only will its surface stop your beads from rolling away, the lack of loops in the fabric will ensure that your needle won't get stuck as you pick up beads.

42 Scissors and cutters

Essential for cutting your thread, you can use a basic pair of scissors but you will find that a small, sharp pair will enable you to cut your threads closer to your work, giving you a neater finish. You can now also purchase thread cutters that can be worn around the neck and keep the blades at a safe distance.

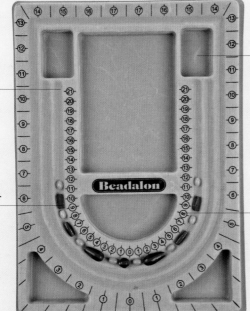

The grooves on a bead board are for you to place beads in, helping you to plan your strands.

Plan multistrand pieces using more than one groove at a time.

Hold beads and findings in the useful indentations to keep everything together.

Use the measurements to work out exact lengths.

A thread cutter can be worn around your neck like a pendant for ease of use.

Small, sharp scissors will give you a closer, neater cut.

43
Files

Smoothing the end of your wire is essential if it's going to rub against your skin or go through your ear. You can purchase special files for this job or even use an emery board. Also available are cup burrs (also called burr cups) which are ideal for rounding the ends of your wire.

From top to bottom: metal file, wire rounder, cup burr, emery board.

45
Loom

This tool is made in different sizes and the size you buy will influence the size you can make your finished pieces. You will only need a loom if you plan to do loom work (see pages 136–144).

44
Thread Zap or lighter

This tool, the end of which heats up on demand, is ideal for burning away unsightly thread ends; you can also use a lighter. Whichever you choose, make sure you only burn away the thread you want to!

46
Glue

Whether it's for gluing beads onto illusion cord, adding end beads to your memory wire, or securing the knots in your elastic, the right glue for the job will make your life a lot easier.

Read the label on your glue carefully to ensure it will glue the materials you have in your stash.

TRY IT

47 Traveling thread holder and cutter

An old dental floss container is ideal to hold your thread and provides a built-in cutter for you.

48 Measuring tape

Accurate measuring at all stages of jewelry designing and making will give you the best result.

49 Hammer and block

If you want to add texture to your wirework then you need to get hammering. The type of hammer you're looking for has one flat head and one rounded. A steel block is necessary in order for the hammering to be effective.

Wax will protect your thread, but don't add too much as it may clog up the holes in your beads.

50 Wax and conditioner

Coat your thread in wax or conditioner to get the right tension for the piece you're working on.

51 Magnetic board

This is ideal for holding beading instructions as you work. Place your pattern on the magnetic board and position a magnetic ruler or placeholder on top to keep track of where you are at all times.

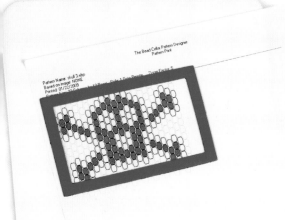

52 EZ Sizers

If you want to make sure your jewelry fits the person it's intended for, you have to take the size of your beads into account. Using an EZ Sizer will help you to get the right size when worn. Simply assemble your EZ Sizer and place your work-in-progress on top. You will be able to see the true wearable size and length from where each design sits.

Pliers and wire cutters

There is a huge variety of pliers and wirework tools on the market. Choosing which ones to buy is made easier by knowing how each one differs and the type of work they can be used for.

SEE ALSO:

Turned loops, page 74
Wrapped loops,
page 76
Making a coil, page 80
Adding texture,
page 84
Cutting and filing wire,
page 72

53 Wire cutters

There are two main types of wire cutters: side cutters and end cutters. The difference is where the cutting surface lies. The most commonly used are side cutters and because of this they're often sold simply as "cutters." You will also come across the term "flush" or "semi-flush" cutters. This refers to how smooth and flat the ends of the cut wire will be after use.

SIDE CUTTERS
Side cutters are the most commonly available and the most useful, as the neat position of their cutting surface enables you to get in close to your work.

END CUTTERS
End cutters are usually stronger than side cutters and are perfect for working with thicker metals.

54 Pliers

Whether you use these to fasten cord endings, crimp beads, or make loops, it's always useful to have a pair of flat-nose and round-nose pliers to hand.

CRIMPING PLIERS
Although not designed as a wirework tool, these can be invaluable in getting a great finish on your wrapped loops. The rounded notch in the jaws fits over your cut wire end and smooths it out. These are perfect if you plan on doing a lot of crimping and want the best results. They have two notches in the jaws which are designed to squash and then shape your crimp beads.

FIX IT

55 Serrated jaws

Never use pliers that have serrated jaws. These will grip into your wire, marking it and ruining the look. If these are all you have to hand, you can wrap masking tape around the jaws as a temporary measure.

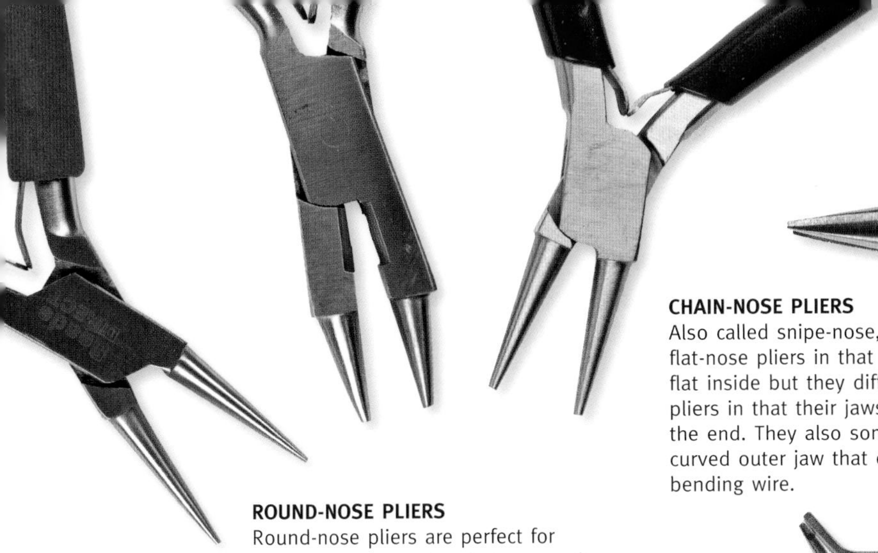

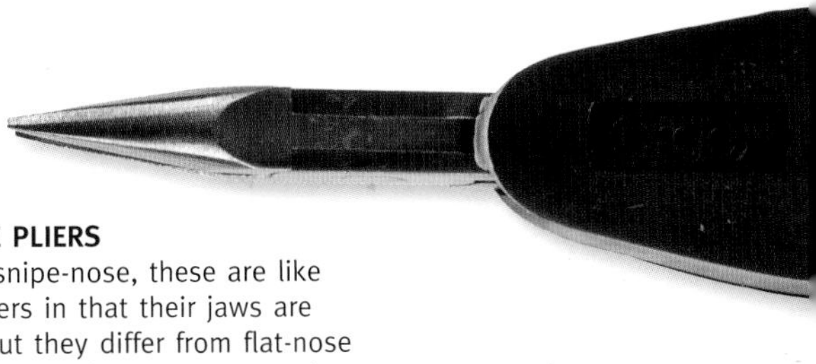

CHAIN-NOSE PLIERS

Also called snipe-nose, these are like flat-nose pliers in that their jaws are flat inside but they differ from flat-nose pliers in that their jaws taper toward the end. They also sometimes have a curved outer jaw that can be used for bending wire.

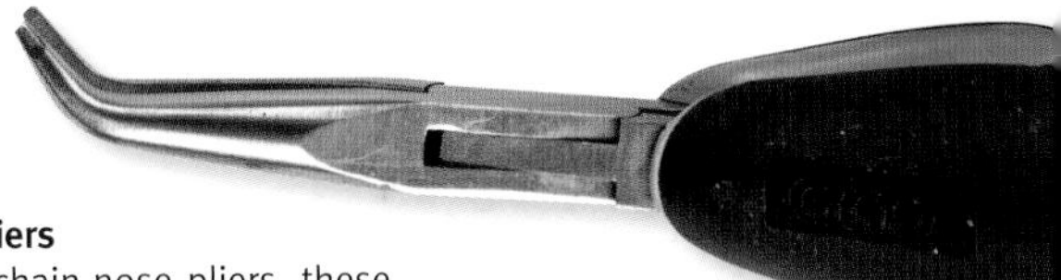

Bent-nose pliers

A variant of chain-nose pliers, these bend toward the end. This can enable you to get them into tricky places to help hold your work.

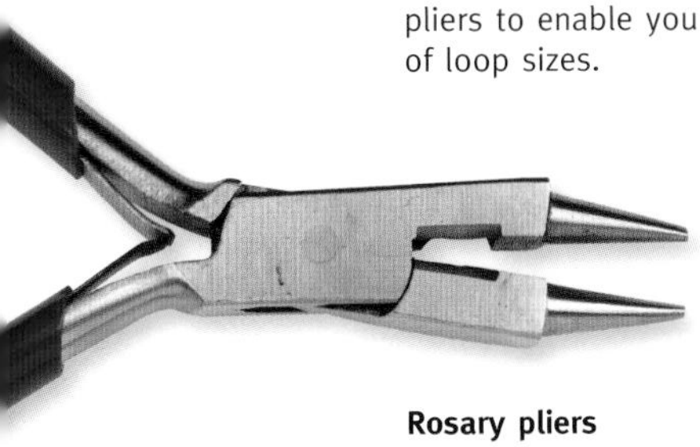

ROUND-NOSE PLIERS

Round-nose pliers are perfect for forming loops and bends in your wire. Their jaws taper toward the end, and whereabouts you place your wire on the jaw determines the size of the loop you'll make. Once you get started with wirework you may find you want to build up a collection of different-sized pliers to enable you to make a variety of loop sizes.

Rosary pliers

Keep an eye out for round-nose pliers with an integrated side cutter. These are called rosary pliers as they enable you to make turned loops or rosary units (see page 74) with just one pair of pliers.

Three-step pliers

These pliers, with their three different-sized "steps," are perfect for making the same-sized loops again and again. You may find them trickier to use at first as they don't have a spring and therefore don't bounce back as you're using them.

FLAT-NOSE PLIERS

So-called because their jaws are flat inside. These differ from chain-nose pliers in that the width of their jaws stays the same all the way along. These are ideal for holding and bending wire.

Nylon-jawed pliers

Whether it's got a curve from being on a reel or kinked through use, wire can get easily twisted. These pliers are ideal for straightening out all those curves and kinks without marking your wire. Grip the end of your wire using flat- or chain-nose pliers or using your hand (shown below) and run a pair of nylon-jawed pliers along the wire length for a great, straight result.

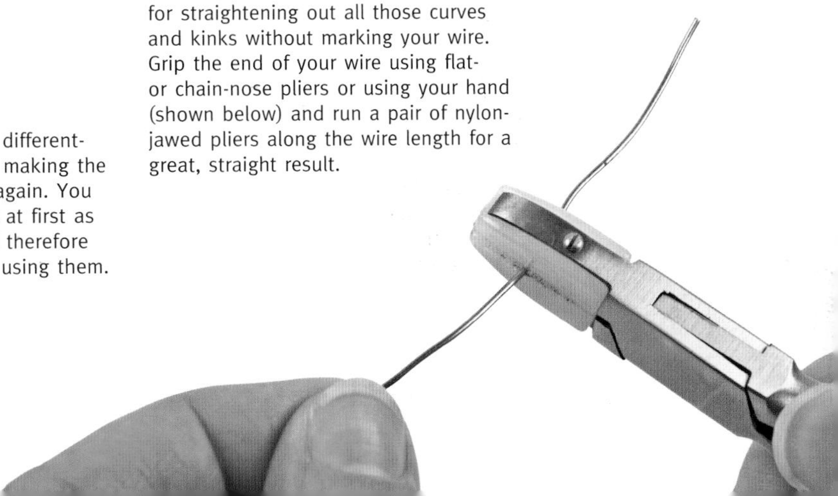

Storage

Once you start building up your bead stash, you'll soon need to find ways of storing it all. There are lots of different solutions out there and each one may be suitable for a different reason. Read on for some help in making your choices.

SEE ALSO:

Beginning with beads, page 10
Essential findings, page 40
Useful extras, page 42

56

Bead storage

Will you be beading in one room or at a bead group or class? Will you be storing small seed beads or large gemstones, big reels of wire and tools, or small reels of thread and packs of needles? How about decanting your beads? Or finding them a home in a see-through case, to avoid opening the lids or reading the labels? Pick and choose from the below storage options to suit your beads and preferred beading techniques.

SCREW-TOPS
See-through containers that stack and screw together are useful because you can see your beads easily.

HOMEMADE
You may find that you don't need to purchase storage at all. Camera film containers, glass and plastic bottles, flip-top candy packets, and food storage containers can be used as required.

COMPARTMENTALIZE
Boxes with divisions are handy as you can keep a range of beads together. However, make sure you choose a box where the beads stay in separate compartments when the lid is closed. There is nothing worse than organizing your beads only to have them all mix together! Also consider that it may be hard to remove and replace your beads without accidentally mixing them in with the beads in the next section.

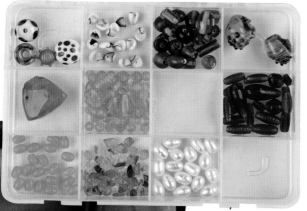

CARRY CASE
A carry case is useful if you plan to visit classes or bead groups and need to take beads with you. When buying one, consider whether you'll also want to carry tools, or books and instructions, and whether you want one to carry or pull along.

FLIP-TOP CONTAINERS
Flip-top containers are available in lots of different sizes and can be used to decant beads into. However, some of them have a lot of static and it can be hard to get all your beads out.

FIX IT

57 To decant or not to decant

Decanting your beads means removing them from the packs, bags, and tubes they were originally purchased in. While this may be easier to store, it means you have to make sure you keep a record of where the beads came from, their color and code, and if you want to buy more of them in the future.

58 Tool storage

Keeping your tools safely stored where they won't get damaged (or damage anything else) is important. A paintbrush holder available from art suppliers is a handy solution.

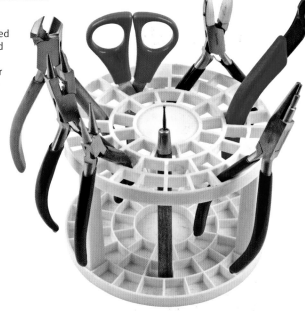

59 Threads

As well as beads, you'll need to work out a solution to store all of those extras such as threads. Keep a range of bobbins on a large stitch holder, usually used in knitting, so they're always handy.

60 How to organize your beads

When planning your storage, you'll need to bear in mind how you want to organize and separate your beads. Do you want to organize them by size? Shape? Color? Material? These decisions will affect the storage you choose.

61 Wire

An expanding file is perfect for holding all your pieces of wire. Separate by size and type.

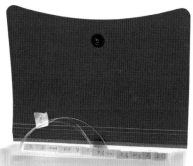

Planning your design

One of the most important things to consider when planning your jewelry is: who will wear it? This is a lot easier when the person is yourself, as you know your tastes and what you're looking for, but it's not so easy when making items for someone else. Read on to learn all about what you need to consider and what to do if you don't know who will buy or wear your jewelry.

SEE ALSO:

Using cord and ribbon, page 60
Using memory wire, page 64
Using elastic, page 63

62

The perfect present

If you know the person you're making the jewelry for, there are lots of things to consider, such as their individual tastes, their body and size, and when the piece might be worn.

Big and bold or small and subtle?
If the wearer loves large, bold necklaces, then trying to please them with a tiny one-strand necklace may not work. Keep asking yourself questions and you'll soon hit upon the right design.

Consider their fashion tastes
Do they wear bracelets? If not, consider making them a watch instead. Do they hate anything tight around their neck? If so, a choker or memory wire necklace isn't right for them. Do they like color? If so, which ones? And what tones would suit their complexion? Some people can wear bold colors, whereas some suit softer, more natural ones. For inspiration, think of clothes you've seen them wear that suit them. High necklines may need a necklace that sits high on the neck or comes down over the clothes. Take all of this into consideration and you'll soon be on your way to making something they'll be delighted with.

Diamante diva or clay-bead commuter?
Is the wearer the type of person who only wears jewelry when they go out, or do they accessorize every day? If it's the latter, you will need to take practical considerations into account. Do they have a practical job where it may be better for jewelry to be easily removed? Is the piece likely to break if caught? Is a certain length better?

Think practical
Does the wearer have pierced ears? If not, you will need to make sure you can use clip-on findings which suit the earring you want to make. Do you know what size their neck or wrist is? If not, consider using elastic or memory wire or adding an extender clasp to anything you make. If they struggle using clasps, then memory wire, elastic, or a magnetic clasp may be the solution. Do they have a pacemaker? If so, don't use a magnetic clasp as it may interfere with it.

If designing for a man, choose your beads and stringing material to suit their tastes and consider when they will wear it.

Memory wire is ideal for anyone who struggles with a clasp or wants to be able to slip their jewelry on and off easily.

63

Men's jewelry

Men wearing jewelry is becoming increasingly popular and gives you a whole new area of design to consider. Some factors you may need to consider are:
Color and contrast: Will he wear the piece with jeans or a suit?
Size and scale: Does he want it to be seen or hidden?
Safety: If he does a physical job, you may want to consider jewelry that will break easily if caught.

FIX IT

66   Size matters

If you don't know the size of the person you're making the jewelry for, or are making pieces to sell, it's best to factor this into the piece. Using elastic and memory wire overcomes most size issues, but these aren't always the most elegant of solutions. If you want to string using cord, crimps, or thread and knots, you can add an extender chain to give the recipient some scope in the wearing length. They also mean one necklace can be worn with different necklines.

Extender chains like these are perfect for making adjustable jewelry.

65

Watches

Making someone a watch is the ideal way to combine the decorative with the practical. A watch is just the same as other jewelry in that it can be subtle or ostentatious, coordinated or clashing, and may even get a non-jewelry wearer down the path of accessorizing without feeling too showy.

64

Children's jewelry

There are serious safety considerations in making jewelry for children. Children young enough to put items into their mouths should not wear jewelry, especially anything that has small components or might break. But as they get older, children's jewelry should be designed to break easily in case the child is playing and gets the piece of jewelry caught. Because of this, memory wire or elastic are the best materials to use.

If someone doesn't like wearing much jewelry, consider making them a watch instead.

SEE ALSO:

Cords, threads, and memory wire, page 18
Storage, page 28

Designing with color

Color is the first thing that usually strikes us when we see a piece of jewelry. We notice if it's bright, if it's subtle, if it contrasts or blends with what someone is wearing—or with the silver or gold metal clasp used in the design. Color also helps us to identify what the beads are made of, if the piece was intended to make a statement, and if so, what? Color often has meaning and purpose but you need to remember that color can be played with and that ultimately, it comes down to personal taste.

67

Starting with color

Some people can put colors together without even having to think about it, whereas others need to work hard to get a result they're happy with. If you fall into the second category, don't worry, there are lots of tips and tricks to help you find a combination you're happy with. First, let's learn some more about colors.

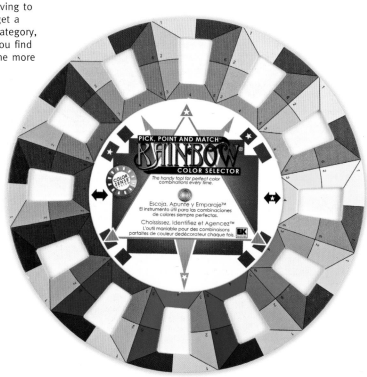

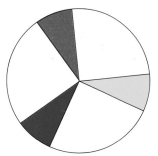

PRIMARY COLORS
These are the main colors: blue, yellow, and red. They are called the primary colors as they cannot be made from any other colors—they are pure color.

SECONDARY COLORS
These are colors made when you mix the primaries: green (from yellow and blue); violet (from red and blue); and orange (from red and yellow).

BLACK AND WHITE
Although technically not colors, black and white are often put in the primary color category as they are basic colors used to enhance others.

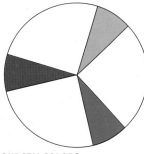

COLOR WHEELS
The best tool to help you with color is a color wheel. It shows all of the primary (red, yellow, blue) and secondary (green, orange, violet) colors. The position of each color on the wheel determines how it reacts with others. Colors opposite each other are called complementary colors. They create striking contrasts when placed side by side.

68

Finding the right combination

There are set color combinations and theories on combining colors, the rules of which can help you to make choices. Practice beginning with a specific bead and follow the rules to see what combinations you can come up with that appeal to you.

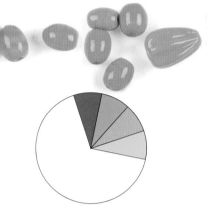

CHOOSE A STARTING COLOR
These orange beads (left) are perfect for experimenting with—orange is a very strong color that most people shy away from using as they don't know where to begin with it.

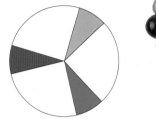

ANALOGOUS COLOR SCHEMES
These schemes use two or more colors that sit next to each other on the color wheel. Here this means matching the orange beads with yellows, and reds with oranges, all of which work together to tone down the bright orange.

COMPLEMENTARY COLORS
Often also called contrasting colors, this works on the theory that colors opposite each other on the color wheel work well together—red and green, yellow and violet, and in this case, orange and blue. In complementary combinations both colors work with each other with the result that the orange and blue beads both look very strong.

SPLIT-COMPLEMENTARY
This is your first color combined with the two colors that sit either side of its complementary. In this case it means using green and violet beads in combination with the original orange ones. See how the orange is toned down by the combination.

69

Adding colors in other ways

It's not just beads that you can use to make the color combinations you want. Remember that the metals, findings, and stringing materials you choose should all be taken into account.

Do you prefer green beads on green cord or a mix of green and purple cords?

Would you prefer these orange beads toned down on a matching cord (analogous color scheme) or contrasted, as shown, on a blue cord (complementary)?

Carnelian beads combine with copper for an analogous combination.

Mixing turquoise beads with copper wirework coils on a memory wire band makes use of complementary colors.

Purple glass beads tied onto yellow cord makes use of a complementary combination.

70 Rules are made to be broken

Don't forget that although the rules are there to help you, they can also be broken. A complete mix of colors can work and look fantastic.

72 Themes

Some colors may not obviously go together, but if they are themed in some other way they can be united.

You might not have chosen to mix all of these colors together, but the use of the stripes on the beads helps to unite them.

This mix of random but strong colors may have looked messy without the uniting influence of the black beads.

71 Black and white

Black-and-white color combinations are bold and strong. You can add to them with different colors and metals for a whole new look.

Shades can be created by adding silver beads and findings.

Adding a strong color to black and white keeps up the bold theme.

73 Finishes

Beads come in a variety of finishes, some of which are more permanent than others. Glass, pearl, and semi-precious beads can be dyed, but be careful as the dye may stain your skin or clothes. If you are unsure about the longevity of a finish, it is always best to test it before you use the beads. You can put the beads into warm water and then dry them with a white fabric or tissue to see if there's any color leakage. Any bead supplier should be able to tell you about the color fastness of the beads they sell you.

74 Shiny versus matte

As beaders and jewelry makers we're often drawn to shiny things, but beware of using too much shine in your pieces. When the eye sees something shiny, it can be overwhelming; it immediately searches for something matte. If you don't include anything matte, people's eyes may get restless and they will not see the true beauty of your work.

75

Colors with meaning

Colors often come with meaning and symbolism attached to them. If you want to make a piece of jewelry with meaning behind it, then check the list below:

Colors of the rainbow
Red, orange, yellow, green, blue, indigo, and violet.

Birthstones
If you want to make a present for someone and don't know where to start, look up their birthstone for a truly personal present. Remember, you don't have to use the actual gemstone but could instead use a glass bead or crystal of the appropriate color.

January Garnet	July Ruby
February Amethyst	August Peridot
March Aquamarine	September Sapphire
April Diamond	October Opal
May Emerald	November Topaz
June Pearl	December Turquoise

Chakras
The Eastern philosophical and spiritual system features a color structure similar to the rainbow colors: red (base of spine); orange (lower abdomen); yellow (below chest); green (center of chest); blue (throat); indigo or violet (center of forehead); violet or white (top of head).

76

Finding good color combinations

There are lots of sources out there for great color combination ideas.

Look around at what Mother Nature has created and see if you can gain inspiration from natural color themes.

Magazine designers and advertisers spend a lot of time ensuring they choose color combinations that work together. Flick through magazines, tear out any that catch your eye, and keep a scrapbook. When you're looking for future inspiration look through them to see which ones will fit the project you're doing or give you ideas to match colors to the beads you want to use.

Paint manufacturers produce color charts which you can collect and use as a guide to and inspiration for different combinations.

Fabric and wrapping paper both have color combinations and patterns that can serve as inspiration.

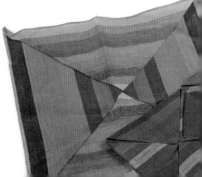

SEE ALSO:

Beginning with beads,
page 10
Planning your design,
page 30

Designing necklaces and bracelets

Necklaces and bracelets are eternally popular and can be made in an endless variety of styles and sizes. Whether you're making a classic one-strand pearl necklace, a floaty illusion necklace, or a bold cord and knot piece, the same considerations need to be made.

Simply stringing beads one after the other highlights their natural pattern.

You can add texture by embellishing a base with smaller beads.

Combining colored beads with silver wire works a treat.

String a mixed bag of beads of the same property and color on memory wire for quick results that look great.

77 Necklace considerations

Give some thought to the following before you launch into your necklace design:

Length: If you're unsure where to start, there are many common lengths that you can take a cue from, and they all have different benefits. Cast an eye over tip 79, opposite, to get some good ideas.

The recipient: Always keep the wearer's preferences, personality, and size in mind.

The beads: The last consideration needs to be your beads. Do you want a single strand of small pearls? A strand of large gemstones? Will you use more than one type of bead—if so, do you want a random or structured pattern? Is there a pendant to hang at the front? Do you need to consider the weight of beads you want to hang at the front?

78 Bracelet considerations

It is the girth and not the length that is the determining factor of a successful bracelet. Here are some other important considerations:

Slip-on or clasp-up? Will your bracelet have a clasp, and if so which kind (see page 41)? Or would the design work undisrupted without one? Memory wire, elastic, and wirework can all be used to make slip-on bracelets.

Size matters: How wide do you want to make the bracelet before comfort becomes an issue?

Working conditions: Does the recipient work at a keyboard? If so the bracelet may receive constant knocks and will need to be able to stand up to this or be made with small beads that won't be as noisy.

Bracelet variations: Is a bracelet the ideal choice? If the recipient doesn't wear a lot of jewelry, a watch may be a better gift.

Necklace lengths

Standard necklace lengths have names and traditions that go back many years. Make your choice depending on the piece you're making and the recipient. Remember that the size of the person will affect the length when worn.

Collar or choker
12–16in (30–41cm)
Not recommended for anyone who doesn't like tight necklaces.

Princess
17–19in (43–48cm)
Ideal for pendants as they will sit high on the chest.

Matinee
20–24in (51–61cm)
Perfect for wearing over a collar or high neckline.

Opera
28–34in (71–86cm)
Ideal for wearing over high-neck or roll-neck tops. Can be worn as a single strand or a multistrand necklace.

Ropes
Over 45in (138cm)
Long and dramatic. Can be worn single, double, or even tripled if long enough.

Adding extra links of metal means each bead can be seen and appreciated.

Adding texture

Texture can be added with both the beads you use and the materials you combine with them. Mix soft and hard to emphasize or play down the different textures you choose.

A bracelet made with felt beads, embellished with seed beads, and then strung on elastic is an attractive option.

Handmade felt beads look softer when strung and spaced out on a metal base.

You don't have to add beads all the way round the string or cord. If using a decorative cord, let this shine through in the finished design.

Designing earrings

SEE ALSO:

Cords, threads, and
memory wire, page 18
Storage, page 28

Never mind a smile, lots of people think a woman is never
fully dressed without her earrings! The act of getting your
ears pierced is often a rite of passage, but many people
end up wearing one style of earring only. By searching for
the right findings and designing with the right techniques
and beads, you'll soon invent new and diverse styles.

81 Planning earrings

There are lots of considerations when
planning a pair of earrings:

Clipped or pierced?
This needs to be your first consideration
as many women do not have their ears
pierced and aren't always catered for. If
you're making earrings for someone and
aren't sure if they have pierced ears, or
are making them to sell, try to come up
with a design where the findings can
easily be swapped.

Metal allergy
Lots of people are allergic to base
metals or can only wear real gold or
silver. Take this into consideration, and
if making earrings to sell, always have
other findings that can be used instead
if required.

Weight
Unlike bracelets or necklaces, the weight
of the beads you use in earrings is far
more important. Carefully consider large
beads, but if they're the size you want
to work with, why not consider using
different materials such as plastic or a
lightweight wood?

Length
Studs and drops are the easiest to wear
as they are unobtrusive and won't get
tangled with the wearer's hair. However,
dangles can be lovely—if you make sure
they're the right length.

Hairstyle and glasses
If someone always wears their hair
down, they may not appreciate large
chandelier earrings that could get caught
up easily. Similarly, people who wear
glasses often don't like fussy earrings
that can clash with bold frames.

Face shape
An elongated face may look even longer
if wearing very long dangles; similarly,
a round face may not suit large hoops.
Consider the face shape of the recipient
when planning earrings, but don't be
limited by it. Some people can carry off
all types of styles no matter what their
face shape or size.

Dinner date or day-to-day?
Some jobs require subtle jewelry,
whereas going out for a fancy dinner
date may call for big and bold.

82 Movement

When designing a piece, you can build in
movement so that, as the wearer moves, so
do elements of their jewelry, catching the light
and adding a new dimension to the work.

When designing earrings, always consider
what other jewelry might be worn. If the
earrings have enough "wow-factor" (as in
the top two photos) they may not need
anything else. If married with an ornate
necklace (as in the bottom photograph),
simple matching earrings will lend style
and will not detract from the centerpiece.

83

Earring styles

There are four main earring styles, with endless variations on each one.

STUDS

Studs are the simplest, smallest, and most subtle form of earring. Comprised of an earring post, they can be all metal or have half-drilled pearls, stones, or beads glued onto them.

DROPS AND DANGLES

From the smallest one-bead drop to long chains and dangles, these earrings can be endlessly played around with so feel free to experiment with beads, charms, and chain.

HOOPS

Round metal hoops range from the tiny and unobtrusive, to those large enough to touch the shoulder. They can be a plain band of metal, have beads threaded onto them, or come with loops on which to attach beads, dangles, or charms.

CHANDELIERS

Chandelier earrings are perfect for anyone who likes to add movement, shape, and color to their jewelry. Look out for chandelier findings that can be combined with your beads and wirework to create bold and beautiful pieces.

TRY IT

84 Think outside the box

Why not play around with conventional earring design and consider decorating the butterflies and backs of your earrings. Try using beads on turned loops attached to pieces of chain to hang from the earring back. This means you can keep the front of the earring plain, but mix and match with different backs. Simply swapping the backs would give you a whole new pair of earrings!

TRY IT

85 Matching sets

When making a special piece of jewelry, always try to make a pair of earrings to match. If you sell your pieces, this could win you lots of extra sales and if it's a gift, the recipient may be able to wear the earrings more often than the rest of the set but always be reminded of your generosity and creativity.

Essential findings

Findings are those little pieces, usually made of metal, that help you to finish your jewelry. These can be clasps, earring hooks, end cones, or even mobile phone charm hangers.

SEE ALSO:

Designing necklaces and bracelets, page 36
Designing earrings, page 38
Useful extras, page 42
Crimping, page 52

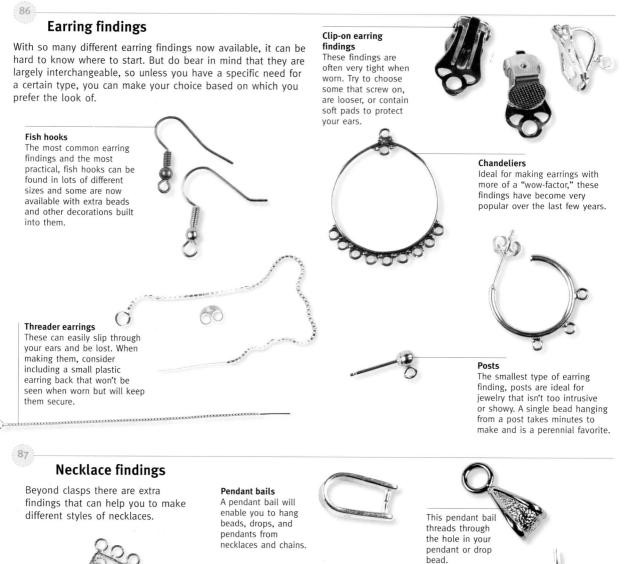

86

Earring findings

With so many different earring findings now available, it can be hard to know where to start. But do bear in mind that they are largely interchangeable, so unless you have a specific need for a certain type, you can make your choice based on which you prefer the look of.

Clip-on earring findings
These findings are often very tight when worn. Try to choose some that screw on, are looser, or contain soft pads to protect your ears.

Fish hooks
The most common earring findings and the most practical, fish hooks can be found in lots of different sizes and some are now available with extra beads and other decorations built into them.

Chandeliers
Ideal for making earrings with more of a "wow-factor," these findings have become very popular over the last few years.

Threader earrings
These can easily slip through your ears and be lost. When making them, consider including a small plastic earring back that won't be seen when worn but will keep them secure.

Posts
The smallest type of earring finding, posts are ideal for jewelry that isn't too intrusive or showy. A single bead hanging from a post takes minutes to make and is a perennial favorite.

87

Necklace findings

Beyond clasps there are extra findings that can help you to make different styles of necklaces.

Pendant bails
A pendant bail will enable you to hang beads, drops, and pendants from necklaces and chains.

This pendant bail threads through the hole in your pendant or drop bead.

Some bails enable you to easily change your necklaces from single to multistrand pieces.

Fold-over bails need to be glued on.

Clasps

The clasps you use will depend on what you have available, what you or the wearer find easiest to use, what you like the look of, and what suits your design.

A subtle toggle and loop will combine well with any jewelry.

Toggles

Also called "t-bars" or "bar and loops," these clasps are easy to use and come in a wide range of styles to suit your finished design. Turn the bar sideways and thread it through the loop along with the end of the piece. Toggles can only be used if the piece that needs to go through the loop is small enough. This means that they're unsuitable if your necklace or bracelet uses big beads. If you want to use this style of clasp, consider adding some small beads to one or both ends of your piece.

Barrels, torpedoes, or screw clasps

These clasps are almost impossible to do up fully when on bracelets and also easily come undone so they are not recommended unless you absolutely have to use them.

Slider

These clasps come with either loops or a bar, both of which can be used to attach your work or beads to. They also come in different lengths, which is ideal for making subtle or bold jewelry to your taste.

Box clasps

These clasps are ideal for making pieces with more than one strand. If you don't like the shiny metal look, you could wipe over them with some colored nail varnish to match your chosen beads.

Magnetic clasps

These clasps are perfect for anyone who struggles to use a clasp but beware, they can easily attach themselves to metal items, such as grocery carts or bus and train hand rails, and without realizing it you can leave your jewelry behind. They also must not be worn by anyone with a pacemaker.

S-hook clasps

These clasps are easy to do up, which makes them ideal for necklaces, but can more easily come undone when used on bracelets. Why not finish your necklaces with soldered jump rings or split rings and use one s-hook clasp for all your different pieces. You can also have different-sized s-hooks to enable you to adjust the wearing length of a necklace.

Bolt rings

Although secure, unobtrusive, and easy to fasten and open, these are often quite small so someone with mobility problems may struggle with them.

Lobsters

Lobsters are easy to use and can be hooked onto a jump or split ring or even a strung, wirework, or beaded loop on your jewelry. Choose a size and metal that matches your work.

Useful extras

These are all those little findings that make your life as a designer and jewelry maker easier and help you to make professional, attractive, and practical pieces of jewelry.

SEE ALSO:

Essential findings, page 40

89

Split or jump rings

Both of these rings of metal can be used to attach other findings to your jewelry. The one you choose will depend on your preference of ease over security.

Soldered jump rings
These give you the look of a solid ring and the security of a split ring. They don't open or close, so you will need to thread through them.

Jump rings
These are small rings of metal which are a lot easier to open and close than split rings but can be pulled apart, so are less secure. Their ease of opening and closing makes them perfect for making chains, attaching dangles, and joining earrings together where security isn't so important.

Split rings
These are coils of metal (like a key-ring), which are harder to open than jump rings but cannot be pulled apart, so are much more secure. Use them as one end of a clasp with a lobster or trigger clasp, or use them to attach a clasp to a bracelet.

90

Head- or eyepins

Each of these pins looks similar and performs the same function—they stop your beads falling off—but the different ends can be used for different purposes. If you want simply to make dangles and stop your beads from falling off, then choose a headpin; if you want to hang something else from it, choose an eyepin with its ready-made loop.

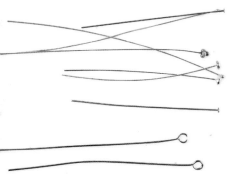

Headpins are lengths of wire with a stop at the end to prevent your beads from falling off.

Eyepins are similar to headpins but have a loop at one end that you can use to hang beads from.

91

Calottes

Also called clamshells or necklace tips, these findings come with a hinge either at the side or at the bottom. Experiment to see which one you find easier to use with your technique or design. You can choose between those with a ready-formed loop, or those where you turn the loop yourself. Calottes with a hinge at the bottom can make it harder to finish the second end of your piece neatly, but this is a personal preference.

AND MORE...

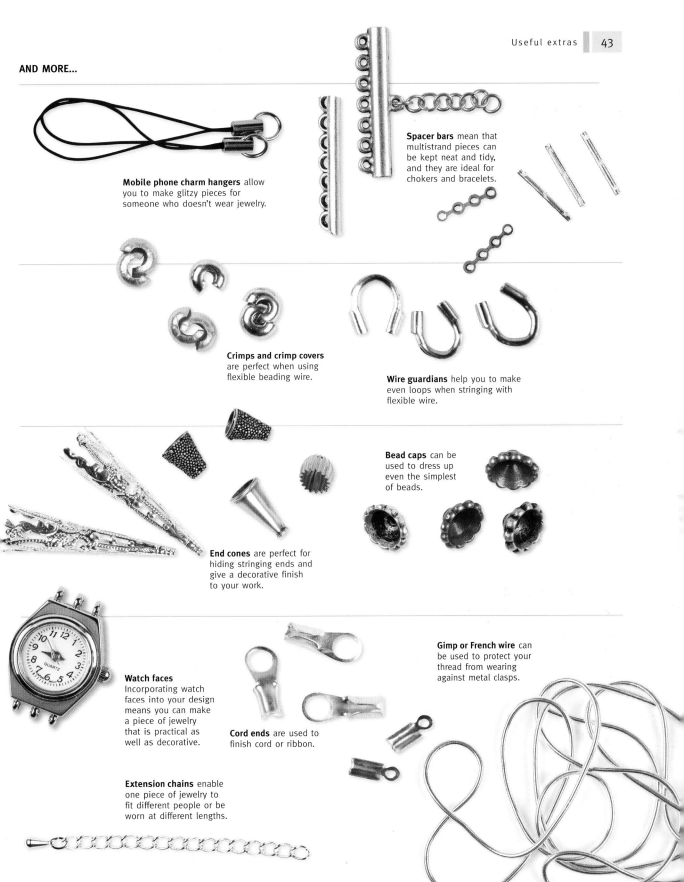

Mobile phone charm hangers allow you to make glitzy pieces for someone who doesn't wear jewelry.

Spacer bars mean that multistrand pieces can be kept neat and tidy, and they are ideal for chokers and bracelets.

Crimps and crimp covers are perfect when using flexible beading wire.

Wire guardians help you to make even loops when stringing with flexible wire.

End cones are perfect for hiding stringing ends and give a decorative finish to your work.

Bead caps can be used to dress up even the simplest of beads.

Watch faces
Incorporating watch faces into your design means you can make a piece of jewelry that is practical as well as decorative.

Cord ends are used to finish cord or ribbon.

Gimp or French wire can be used to protect your thread from wearing against metal clasps.

Extension chains enable one piece of jewelry to fit different people or be worn at different lengths.

Getting comfortable

When settling down to make jewelry, comfort needs to be a top priority. Whether this is ensuring you sit comfortably, work in good light, or just gather all you need at the start, the following tips will help you to work better and guarantee that you end up with great jewelry, not aches and pains.

SEE ALSO:

Cords, threads, and memory wire, page 18
Storage, page 28

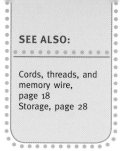

92 Seating position

If you plan on sitting and making jewelry for long periods of time, how you sit is very important.

Posture
Make sure your work is high enough that you don't have to lean over while working. Sitting at a table or with your work and materials on a tray on your lap helps with this.

Back support
Choose a chair with back support and add a cushion if needed. Sitting on a stool or low-backed chair can result in backache.

93 Take a break

As you work, take frequent breaks and run through the following list to ensure you finish each jewelry-making session as fresh as when you started it.
• Stretch and uncurl all the parts of your body that have begun to curl up. This is usually your fingers and hands, back and shoulders, and even your neck.
• Walk around to get your blood flowing again.
• Rest your eyes by focusing on different things and even close them for a while.
• Grab a drink. It's easy to get dehydrated without realizing it and this will affect your concentration and physical ability.

94 Rest your eyes

Jewelry making and beading can be very tiring on your eyes. All that looking at shiny, small items, and concentrating and focusing on one spot will tire and hurt your eyes. Make sure that you frequently look up and away from your work. Look across the room and focus on other items at different distances to stop your eyes becoming sore. Always work in good light to further reduce strain.

95 Care for your hands

Your hands are your most important tools and need to be treated as such. Long periods of time spent jewelry making or wire working without resting them will cause them to be sore and cramped. Take frequent breaks and put down your tools. Stretch your fingers and hands as they may be tight from holding onto pliers and tools. At the end of the day, treat yourself by applying hand cream to help you wind down and restore your hands for your next jewelry-making session.

TRY IT

96 Setting an alarm

If you keep finding yourself caught up in what you're doing, then why not set an alarm on a clock or your phone and leave it on the other side of the room. Every time it goes off you'll be forced to get up and turn it off, thus getting you moving again.

TRY IT

97 Labeling seed beads

When using seed beads and following a pattern, it can be easy to lose track of which beads are which. Try adding stickers to a palette identifying the beads by their number or A, B, C depending on the pattern.

98

Work surface

The ideal work surface is what feels most comfortable to you. Some people prefer to work up at a table, whereas others prefer to sit in a chair with a tray on their lap. Whichever you choose, you'll want to protect the surface while also stopping your beads from rolling away. The ideal solution is a bead mat (see page 23). These are cheap and convenient as your beads won't roll away and, unlike towels or some fabrics, there are no loops for your needles or tools to snag on.

99

Gather and organize your beads

Before you start work, try to think of all the things you will need for the project you're working on. Gathering them all at the start will not only save you time but also make your work better as you won't be tempted to make do with the tools or materials you have on hand, rather than those you should be using.

Arranging your materials

Think about how you want your beads around you. You can keep them in their packets and take out those you need as and when you need them; organize them in little piles; or keep them separated in a bead tray or palette. The option you choose may depend on what you're making or what technique you're using. Here are some recommended arrangements:

• For stringing, having all your beads out may help you to come up with combinations you hadn't thought of.
• When seed beadweaving, you won't want to get your beads mixed up. You may also be more likely to work with color, so a palette might be the perfect choice to keep those colored seed beads apart.

Some lights and bulbs will alter the perceived color of your beads. Always try to examine your beads in good natural light when making your choices.

100

Lighting

Good lighting is important for many reasons. Not only does it help you to see the true colors of your beads and materials, but it will also reduce any strain on your eyes. Always work in good lighting, natural if possible, and make sure you rest your eyes from time to time.

101

Magnification

If you need glasses, make sure you wear them—don't sit and strain your eyes needlessly. Also, consider using another magnification aid to save you squinting. You can find all sorts of items in bead and craft stores—try them out and choose which one you feel most comfortable with.

Stringing

Stringing is the most popular method of jewelry making and can be used to create an endless variety of beautiful beaded creations. The wide range of materials, findings, and stringing techniques can be overwhelming for a beginner, so read on to learn all you need to help you create your best design.

SEE ALSO:

Cords, threads, and
memory wire,
page 18
Storage, page 28

Making aesthetic choices

The first obstacle when it comes to stringing is what to use—both material
and technique. There are lots of reasons why you might want to go with one
over the other. It could be that you're using heavy beads, that you want a
certain look, or that the finished piece is for someone who can't use a clasp.
Use the guidance shown to help you make your decision.

Elastic is ideal
for children and
adults of all sizes,
as pieces can be
easily slipped
on and off.

Cord and ribbons look
great and add a decorative
touch to complement your
choice of beads.

102

Choosing your stringing material

MATERIAL AND TECHNIQUE	PROS	CONS
Flexible beading wire and crimps	• Quick and easy • Can take heavy beads or ones with rougher holes • Can be hidden or on show • Ideal for beads with large or small holes	• Neat crimps can be hard to master—you may want to hide them using extra materials • Requires special tools
Thread and knots	• Knotting has a variety of benefits both decorative and practical (see page 56) • Thread is cheap and requires no expensive or bulky tools	• Can be trickier to do and takes a lot longer • Less resistant to wear and tear • Not suitable for very heavy beads or those with sharp holes
Cords, ribbons, and yarns	• Can add a decorative look to your piece • Can be hidden or on show • Quick results	• Not suitable for beads with small holes • Not suitable for beads with sharp edges • More easily broken
Elastic	• Stringing material can be hidden • Size of wearer not important • Suitable for children or anyone who can't use a clasp	• Can be difficult to get a neat result
Memory wire	• Size of wearer not important • Quick results • Can be hidden or on show • Suitable for children or anyone who can't use a clasp	• Some people don't like tight necklaces • Finished jewelry has no movement or drape to it • Ending with loops is a hard technique to master

Whether you choose to knot or not, using thread results in a finished piece with lots of drape and movement.

Flexible beading wire with crimps is ideal for use with heavy gemstones.

Whether you choose to end your memory wire pieces with loops or caps, they're quick and easy to make.

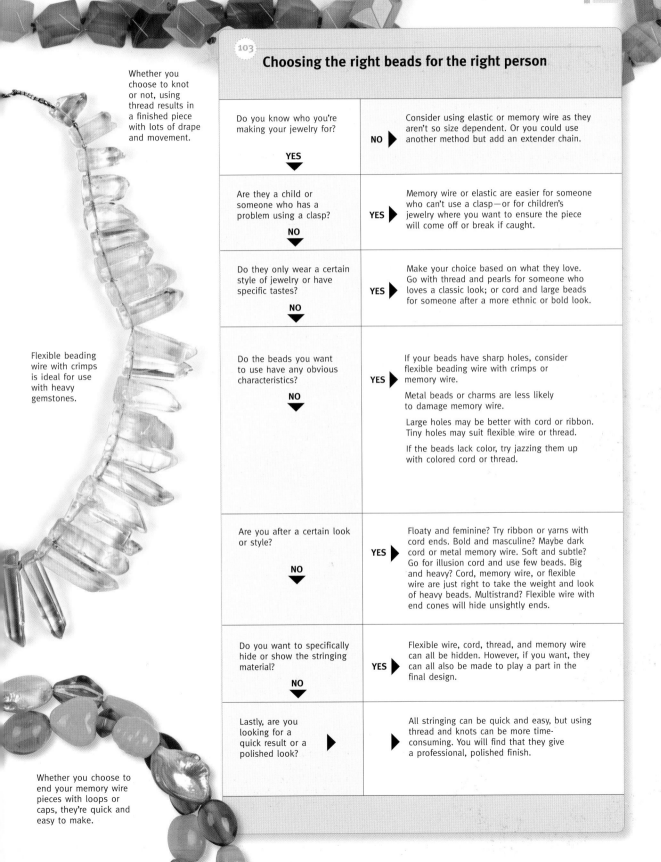

103

Choosing the right beads for the right person

Do you know who you're making your jewelry for? **YES**	**NO** ▶	Consider using elastic or memory wire as they aren't so size dependent. Or you could use another method but add an extender chain.
Are they a child or someone who has a problem using a clasp? **NO**	**YES** ▶	Memory wire or elastic are easier for someone who can't use a clasp—or for children's jewelry where you want to ensure the piece will come off or break if caught.
Do they only wear a certain style of jewelry or have specific tastes? **NO**	**YES** ▶	Make your choice based on what they love. Go with thread and pearls for someone who loves a classic look; or cord and large beads for someone after a more ethnic or bold look.
Do the beads you want to use have any obvious characteristics? **NO**	**YES** ▶	If your beads have sharp holes, consider flexible beading wire with crimps or memory wire. Metal beads or charms are less likely to damage memory wire. Large holes may be better with cord or ribbon. Tiny holes may suit flexible wire or thread. If the beads lack color, try jazzing them up with colored cord or thread.
Are you after a certain look or style? **NO**	**YES** ▶	Floaty and feminine? Try ribbon or yarns with cord ends. Bold and masculine? Maybe dark cord or metal memory wire. Soft and subtle? Go for illusion cord and use few beads. Big and heavy? Cord, memory wire, or flexible wire are just right to take the weight and look of heavy beads. Multistrand? Flexible wire with end cones will hide unsightly ends.
Do you want to specifically hide or show the stringing material? **NO**	**YES** ▶	Flexible wire, cord, thread, and memory wire can all be hidden. However, if you want, they can all also be made to play a part in the final design.
Lastly, are you looking for a quick result or a polished look? ▶	▶	All stringing can be quick and easy, but using thread and knots can be more time-consuming. You will find that they give a professional, polished finish.

SEE ALSO:

Seed beads and more,
page 12
Making aesthetic
choices, page 48

Stringing tips and tricks

Although stringing techniques can be easy to master, a few tips and tricks go a long way in helping you achieve a professional finish.

7in (18cm)

104 · Size matters

Both the bracelets above are 7in (18cm) end to end when laid flat. But when fastened you can see the actual wearable length varies greatly. This is because the size of the beads used will influence the internal circumference. You need to take this into account when making your pieces, and using an EZ Sizer (right) will help you get the correct result.

Before adding your clasp and finishing your work, check the actual wearable length is what you need. The size of beads you use can make an enormous difference to the final length.

Toddler 4"
4 1/4"
4 1/2"
4 3/4"
5"
5 1/4"
5 1/2"
6"
6 1/4"
6 1/2"
6 3/4"
Bracelet 7"
7 1/4"
7 1/2"
7 3/4"
8"
8 1/4"
8 1/2"
8 3/4"
Anklet 9"
9 1/4"
9 1/2"
9 3/4"
10"
10 1/4"
10 1/2"
10 3/4"
11"
11 1/4"
11 1/2"
11 3/4"
12"
12 1/4"
12 1/2"
EZ Bracelet
Patent Pending

106 · Matching materials to beads

A golden rule of stringing is that the holes in your beads are always smaller than you remember, and the stringing material you choose is always thicker than you think. Whenever possible, take whichever one you already have along when you go shopping for the other, and actually test whether they fit together. Simply examining holes from the outside can be misleading.

105 · Finished length

When making a piece to the right size, you need to take all of the components into account. Don't forget that your clasp, jump rings, crimps, etc. will all add length, and not including them in your calculations might mean you make your finished piece too short or long.

1¹⁄₂in (37mm)

Actual size

107 · Let it bend

When finishing a piece, never pull it all so tight that it won't be able to bend and be worn. Although it might look wrong, it's always better to leave a gap that shows when the jewelry isn't worn, as this will accommodate the curve when it is worn.

Make your own needles

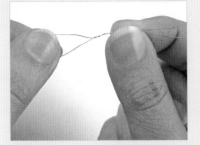 

If you don't have a fine beading needle handy, you can always make your own. Take a piece of very fine wire. Bend it in half and, holding the ends, twist them tightly together,

making sure you leave a space at the bend to act as the eye. It is almost impossible to twist the ends neatly, so do as well as you can and then trim any untwisted pieces.

Stop losing beads

When stringing, sizing, and planning your design, you want the freedom to play around with your work without losing all your beads on the floor. The best way to deal with this is to use a Bead Stopper, paperclip, or knot at the end of your stringing material.

Threading your needle

Try to thread your needle so that you take one cut end through the eye. This means you end up with only two pieces of thread to get through the small holes in your beads. Threading it by putting both cut ends through would mean you have four pieces of thread to pull through.

Testing for security

Always test that your crimp, knot, or cord ending is secure. Do this by gently tugging on it. If it hasn't held, this should be enough to let you know.

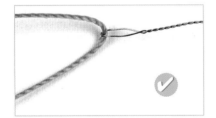 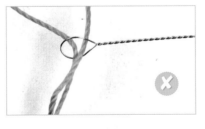 

When laid out flat, this bracelet has a gap but when bent and worn on the wrist, it disappears.

These large crystals would grind against each other and become damaged if not strung with the smaller beads in-between them.

When is a knot not a knot?

If you love the look of knots but don't want to tie them, or if you are using a material that doesn't want to hold a knot, then you can add a small seed bead between your larger beads to give the illusion of a small knot.

Small beads imitate knots and are fairly easy to string.

SEE ALSO:
Jewelry-making tools, page 22
Essential findings, page 40
Making aesthetic choices, page 48
Stringing tips and tricks, page 50

Crimping

Although a fairly modern technique, using flexible wire and crimping is now the most commonly used method of stringing in jewelry making. It's quick to learn, easy to master, and once you know what you're doing, you'll be able to make a piece of jewelry at a moment's notice.

113

What is crimping?

Crimping is essentially squashing a small metal bead so that it bites into the nylon coating of your flexible beading wire and secures your necklace or bracelet. You can use either flat-nose or crimping pliers to crimp—both techniques are described on these two pages.

114

Using flat-nose pliers

Flat-nose pliers will give you a secure crimp but it won't be as attractive as one formed using crimping pliers.

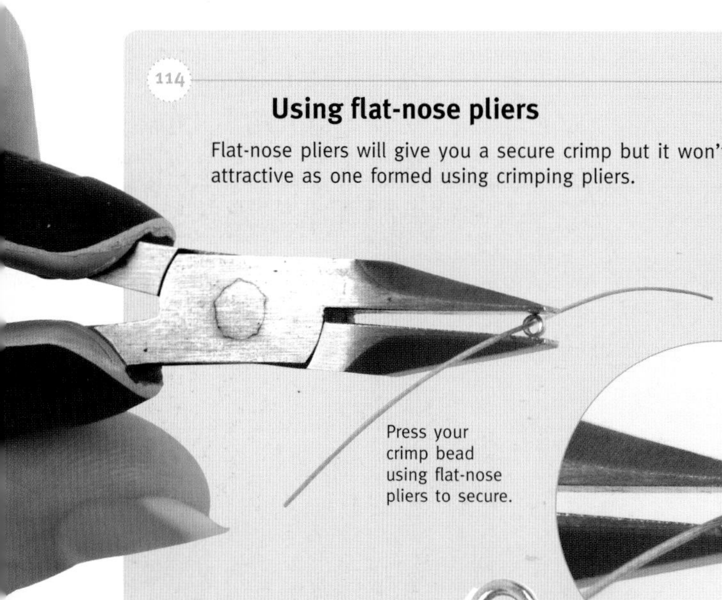

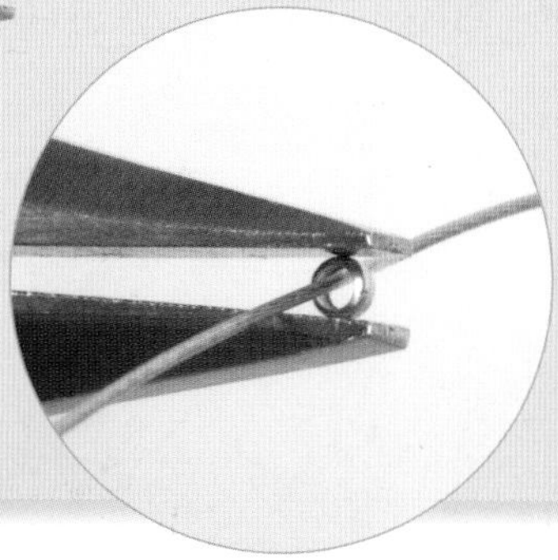

Be careful! Using flat-nose pliers gives you a square crimp with corners that may be sharp.

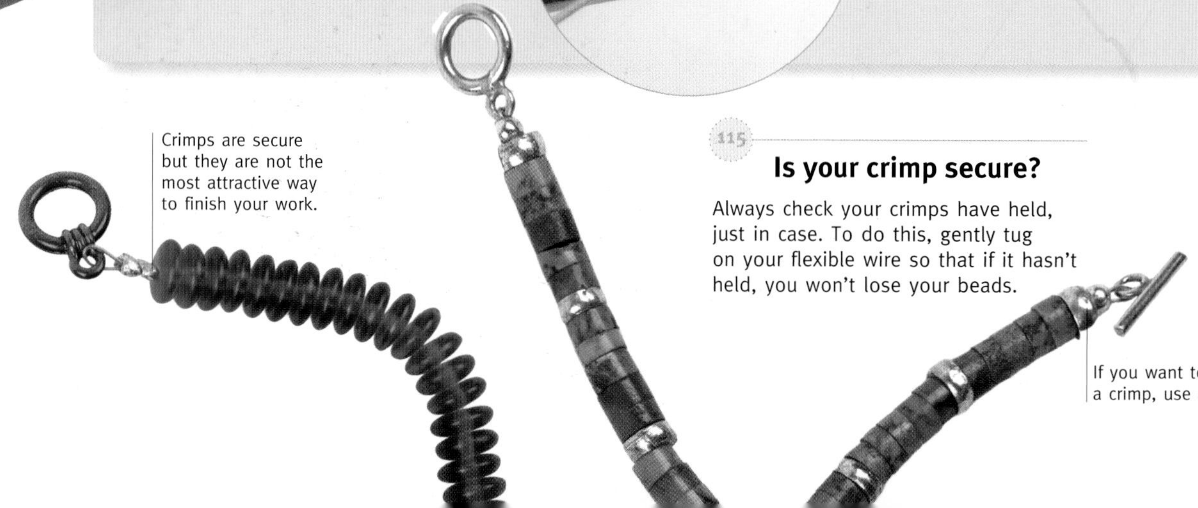

Press your crimp bead using flat-nose pliers to secure.

Crimps are secure but they are not the most attractive way to finish your work.

115

Is your crimp secure?

Always check your crimps have held, just in case. To do this, gently tug on your flexible wire so that if it hasn't held, you won't lose your beads.

If you want to hide a crimp, use a cover.

116

Using crimping pliers

Crimping pliers are specially designed to give you not only a secure crimp, but a more rounded and attractive one.

Always ensure you turn your crimp sideways before giving it its final crimp.

1 Press your crimp first using the notch nearest the handle of your pliers—this crimps the center of the bead and turns your crimp into a figure-eight shape. The aim is to get one piece of flexible wire into each section of the crimp.

2 Move your crimp to the notch nearest the point of your pliers. You now need to turn it so that it sits with one wire above the other. Press down with your pliers to round the crimp. You can then rotate your crimp in the pliers and re-crimp to fully round it.

3 When crimping pliers are used, the end result is a much rounder and neater crimp with no sharp edges.

117

Hiding your crimps

If you don't like the look of crimps, you can hide them using crimp covers. These are sold in a variety of sizes and metals and, when added to your jewelry (and closed), they will look like a small metal bead.

The rounded notch in your crimping pliers is the ideal tool for closing the crimp cover.

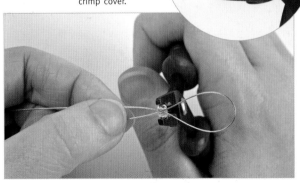

A crimp cover gives the look of a bead and hides the unsightly crimp. It also ensures you won't be scratched by any sharp edges.

Use your crimping pliers to close the crimp cover nicely. You may need to keep adjusting it as you go to ensure the edges line up neatly.

118

Stringing your necklace

It's up to you whether you choose to string from one end to the other or build your piece up from the center. Whichever you choose, make sure you have added a Bead Stopper or paperclip to one end to stop all your beads accidentally falling off.

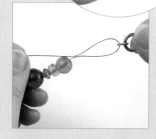

1 Cut a suitable length of flexible beading wire. You want the finished length of your piece plus at least 4in (10cm). String a crimp bead and thread through the attaching loop of your clasp and back down through your crimp bead. Tighten the loop but ensure that the clasp can still move freely. Squash your crimp bead and check it is secure.

2 Begin to string your piece, making sure your beads cover both pieces of wire. Continue to string until you have added all the beads you want to use.

3 Thread on a crimp bead and the attaching loop of the other end of your clasp. Thread back down through the crimp bead and some of the beads in your piece.

4 Pull your flexible wire tight so that your clasp cannot freely move. Beware from this point, as you have not yet secured your crimp bead and there's still a risk of it coming undone. To reduce the risk, try and keep the piece on your work surface so its own weight won't pull it undone.

119

One crimp or two?

How many crimps you use is your choice. However, using an extra one on each side will cover you just in case one of them breaks—this is more likely if you are hard on your jewelry or are using large, heavy beads. You can add one crimp, then a bead, and then the second crimp if you want them to be less obvious—and don't forget that covering them with a crimp cover makes them even less noticeable.

FIX IT

120 No crimp covers?

If you don't have any crimp covers, a side-opening calotte can be used instead. Simply cut the attaching loop off as neatly as you can.

5 Trim your flexible wire as close as you can.

6 Return to your clasp and gently loosen it so it can move and so that the cut end of wire is pulled up into the bead for extra security.

7 Crimp the second end as you did the first.

Double check
Before securing your second end, always go back and check that, at the first end, no pieces of wire have worked themselves out of the bead holes.

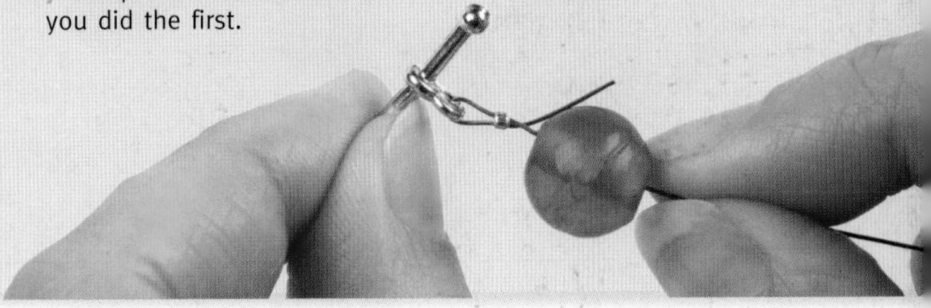

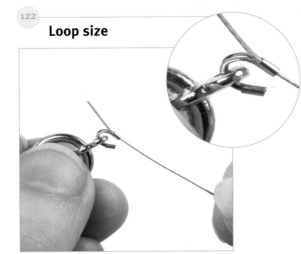

 121

Avoiding wear

If you make your loop too small, the flexible beading wire will rub against your clasp and wear down, resulting in a piece that soon breaks.

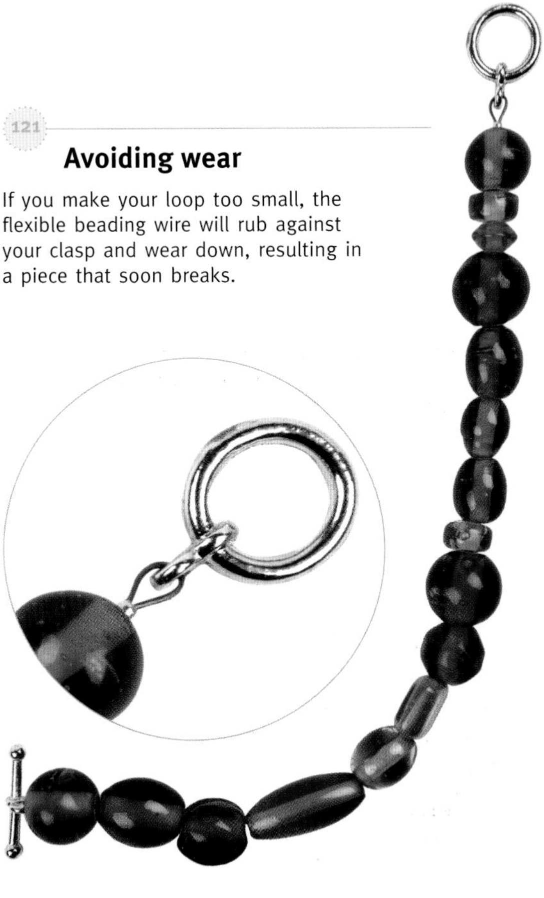

122

Loop size

The size of the loops of flexible wire you leave is your choice, but the ideal size is one that isn't too large and noticeable, while still ensuring your clasp can move freely. If you want to always make the same sized loop and reduce wear, then using a wire guardian is the ideal solution.

Threads and knots

Stringing with thread is the traditional method used for centuries to create beautiful jewelry and is commonly associated with pearl necklaces. It is still used today and there are many different techniques you can employ. The easiest and most effective, using calottes, is described below. If you're in the mood for an advanced technique with a different look, adding gimp might be just what you're looking for.

SEE ALSO:

Jewelry-making tools, page 22
Stringing tips and tricks, page 50
Using cord and ribbon, page 60
Turned loops, page 74
Opening and closing loops, page 82

The knots in this necklace help to frame and highlight each bead. It also creates space between each bead so that the square sides don't stop the necklace from curving when worn. In this way, a longer necklace is achieved with less expense.

123 Why knot?

There are lots of reasons for using knots: they're decorative and can add a touch of color and texture to your piece; they frame each bead so they can be seen as separate things of beauty rather than as one long strand; they can help the way your beads lie in a piece; they can be used to hold beads or charms in place on a strand; and they can also be used to make a few beads go a long way.

124 Using calottes

Begin with a length of thread at least four times the length of the finished piece you want to make (if you're not knotting, it only needs to be double).

1 Thread your needle so you have two pieces of thread exiting the eye.

2 Tie a knot at the end of your thread. You want this to be large enough so it doesn't pull out of the hole in the calotte. Lay the knot in the calotte and close it using a pair of pliers.

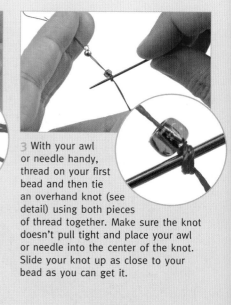

3 With your awl or needle handy, thread on your first bead and then tie an overhand knot (see detail) using both pieces of thread together. Make sure the knot doesn't pull tight and place your awl or needle into the center of the knot. Slide your knot up as close to your bead as you can get it.

FIX IT

125 Bottom-hinged calotte?

If your calotte has a hinge at the bottom, you'll need to take this into account when threading your necklace.

1 Begin by taking your knotted thread down through the bottom so the knot sits in the hole.

2 When finishing your necklace, use your awl or needle to slide your knot into the calotte before trimming the thread.

126 To trim or not to trim?

When placing your knot in the calotte you have two choices:

To trim: Trimming the ends of the thread first gives a neater finish, but it's then harder to handle the thread and close the calotte.

Not to trim: Not trimming makes it easier to place the knot, but harder to trim the thread without any of it showing later.

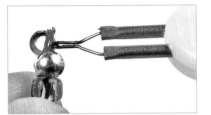

Alternatively, leave the thread ends, close your calotte, trim the ends, and then use a Thread Zap or lighter to get rid of any thread still showing.

128 Securing your knot

If you're worried about your knot sliding through the calotte hole, or the calotte breaking and it coming out, you can knot your threads around a small bead to give you a larger end and glue this, or a simple knot, into the calotte for added security.

FIX IT

127 Big holes?

Some beads you might want to string will come with much larger holes. There are a number of ways you can deal with this:

Use more strands of thread: Instead of two strands, why not try four, six, or eight?

Bigger knots: You can tie two or three knots on top of each other.

Thicker thread: Why not try a thicker thread or even a cord?

Smaller beads: Adding a smaller bead each side of your larger one will mean that the knots will hold in place and not slip through the large holes.

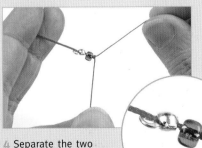

4 Separate the two strands of thread and pull on them to slide your knot up that extra amount needed to place it right next to the bead.

5 Thread on another bead and repeat the same knot-tying process. Continue this until you have added as many beads as required. When tying your last knot, make sure you leave a little space to take your calotte.

6 Add a calotte to the second end as you did the first and then attach a clasp to finish, using jump rings if required.

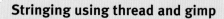

Stringing using thread and gimp

If you're looking for more of a challenge, then you can try stringing using thread and gimp. Essential to this technique is using a fine or homemade needle that can be cut off. This technique is much more complicated than using calottes—because you thread all the beads on first, you cannot alter the length as you go.

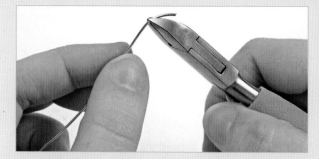

1 Cut a small section of gimp, about ½in (1cm) long, using wire cutters.

129
A weighty issue

As you string your necklace, the weight of the beads will make the piece heavier and can mean that, as you pull the strand through to tie the next knot, it can be pulled tight where you don't want it to sit. Watch out for this and always try to work as close to your work surface as you can—let this take the weight of the beads rather than have them hang down.

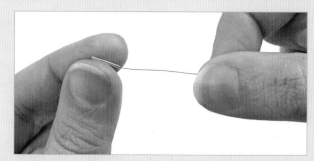

2 Add a fine or homemade needle to a piece of thread at least four times the finished length you want and tie a knot at the other end. Thread on one bead and your piece of gimp.

130
Attaching a clasp

Some calottes come with a ready-made loop and some come with a length of wire for you to form your own loop. Simply make a turned loop using a pair of round-nose pliers and attach this to the clasp of your choice.

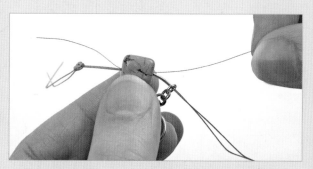

3 Thread through the attaching loop in your clasp and then back down your bead. Don't worry about tightening or neatening this end yet.

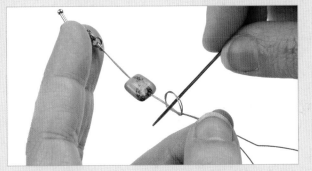

4 String on all your beads, then a piece of gimp the same size as before, and the other end of your clasp. Cut off your needle.

7 With your awl or blunt needle handy, slide one bead down toward the gimp and tie an overhand knot. Place the awl or needle into the knot before it tightens and slide it down as close to the bead as you can get it. Separate the ends of your thread and pull them so the knot slides the rest of the way to the bead.

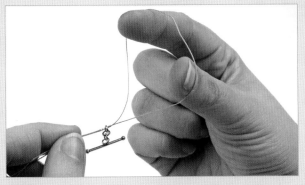

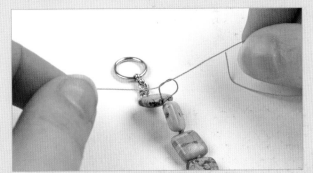

5 Slide the gimp and clasp close to the end loop of thread. Put your fingers through the loop and take hold of your gimp and the clasp. Make sure that the clasp sits on the gimp at all times—this will stop it slipping through.

8 Continue sliding beads and tying knots until you have one bead left. Slide this bead down but don't tie a knot. Gently adjust the bead from the beginning as well as from the gimp and clasp until they are up close to the other beads. Cut the knot from your thread, use the ends to tie an overhand knot, and slide this as close to the beads as you can. Trim the thread as close as you can (using a Thread Zap or lighter if needed) and add a touch of glue to hold the knot and neaten any frayed ends, if required.

6 Pull tight so that the loop of thread catches around the rest of the thread and your gimp bends to sit nicely in your clasp.

SEE ALSO:

Designing with color,
page 32
Essential findings,
page 40
Threads and knots,
page 56
Turned loops,
page 74
Opening and closing
loops, page 82

Using cord and ribbon

Cords and ribbons are the perfect accompaniment to your beads. Variations in shape, color, size, and texture can add a new dimension that is not always possible with just beads.

Knots are used in this necklace as "brakes" to stop the beads and charms from sliding into one another.

132 Knots as brakes

Why not use knots to stop beads or charms from gathering at the center of a necklace? The leather cord necklace above has had lots of beads, shells, and charms threaded on, all separated by knots spaced apart at intervals. Because of the placement of the knots, all the decorations can move around, giving the necklace life.

WEAR AND TEAR
If you add beads or charms to your cords or knots, make sure they're smooth so they don't wear your cord.

HOW IT ALL LIES
Pay attention to how the beads lie in the finished piece. There's no point adding them only for them to sit behind your cords and not be seen.

FIX IT

133 Threading your beads

When using cords and ribbons, it can be tricky to thread on your beads. Try this quick solution.

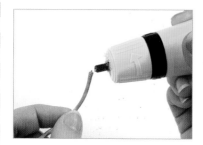

1 Paint the end with glue, squashing it tight while doing so.

2 When dry, trim the cord at an angle to a point. This gives you a smaller end that doesn't flop when you try to thread on a bead.

By using a stripey ribbon, the colors appear to swirl through the knots.

134 Playing with knots

Choose a colored cord that complements or contrasts with your beads, or take it another step by using more than one cord at a time. When using two different-colored cords, you can treat them as one cord, knotting them together to see the colors combine in the knots, or you can alternate, tying one around the other to vary the colors that appear between the beads. A similar result can also be achieved when using a variegated cord—you will see the colors of the knots change as you work along the strand.

String your piece using two different cords and take turns knotting one around the other to mix it up.

Using harmonious color combinations will emphasize the textural qualities of the cord.

As you tie a knot why not place a bead or charm in it for a decorative effect?

Using two different-colored cords gives you a different look that can be used to match lots of different outfits.

Use yarn or cord in contrasting colors and the knots will gradually change color between the beads.

135
Using cord ends

Also called cord crimps or cord findings, these are little metal pieces that are perfect for finishing off your cords, ribbons, or yarns.

1 Lay one end of your cord into the finding. You may find it easier to have some overlapping that you can trim off later. Using a pair of pliers that are flat inside, press one side of the finding in so it holds the cord in place.

2 Press the other side of the finding in so it lies on top of the first. It is very hard to get a neat finish at first, but you will improve with practice. The aim at first is to secure the cord.

3 String your beads and attach another cord finding at the other end. Use jump rings to attach your clasp and finish.

136
Right way up

When attaching a cord crimp, always make sure the loop you'll use to attach your clasp faces away from the main body of your necklace.

137
Using end cones

If you want to add a more decorative look to your jewelry and hide lots of cord, ribbon, and yarn ends, then decorative end cones are perfect. Knot or stitch your material to an eyepin and thread through an end cone. Form a turned or wrapped loop and attach a clasp to finish.

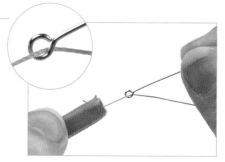

138
More than one strand

Cord ends can take more than one strand of stringing material. Simply place them all in the finding at the same time and close to secure.

139
Trimming cord

When laying the cord into your findings it's a lot easier to leave a piece sticking out of the top of the finding as you hold it. However, this means you'll have to trim the cord afterward, and it's hard to get rid of all the ends. You can use a Thread Zap or lighter to burn away some of the ends— as long as you trim it neatly rather than leave stray bits, it will look well finished.

Using elastic

Commonly used for children's jewelry, beading elastic is now a popular, useful, versatile material that is perfect for making quick, claspless jewelry. It is suitable for making jewelry to sell or for gifts, as sizing is less of an issue.

140 Knotty decision

There are two different knots you can tie to finish your elastic: the overhand knot and the square knot, both of which are outlined below. Each has its own benefits, so make your choice according to your needs.

OVERHAND KNOT
This is the simplest knot to tie, but it's not so easy to hide.

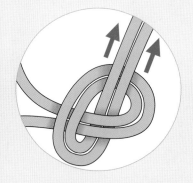

1 Bring the two ends of your elastic together as one. Make sure you remove any excess gaps along the strand of beads.

2 Lay the ends of the elastic over the lengths.

3 Pull the lengths through the hole created. Slide the knot to your work and pull tight to secure.

SQUARE KNOT
Also called a reef knot, this is a variation on a granny knot, with an added element of security.

1 Bring the two ends of your elastic together and lay the left-hand one over the right.

2 Bring what was your left-hand end up through the central space.

3 Take the right-hand end and lay it over the left, then bring it up through the central space.

4 To tighten the knot, you'll have to ensure you get close to it, hold all four "ends" of the elastic, and pull them tight.

FIX IT

141 Finishing your knot

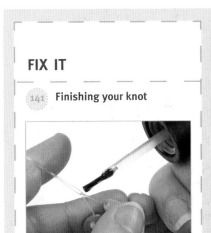

Whichever knot you choose, the best way to finish is to add a touch of superglue to the knot, leave it to dry, and trim the ends close to the knot. Make sure you don't accidentally trim too close or cut your knot.

142 Move that knot

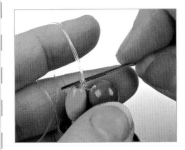

If you find it difficult to get your overhand knot in the right place before it tightens, simply place an awl or a large, blunt needle in the center of the knot and use this to slide the knot closer to where you want it without it tightening.

Using memory wire

Although it looks like a child's toy, memory wire is a useful stringing material. Ideal for use when making children's jewelry or when you don't know the size of the person you want to make something for, memory wire requires no clasp, is quick to use, and is tough enough to stand up to wear and tear.

SEE ALSO:

Planning the design, page 30
Making aesthetic choices, page 48
Cutting and filing wire, page 72
Turned loops, page 74
Making a coil, page 80

143 Buying memory wire

Memory wire is now available in multiple bracelet, ring, and necklace-sized variations and can be bought as single loops or whole coils. Buying a coil is much more economical and also means you can choose the length you want to cut rather than have it dictated.

144 How much to cut?

There's a simple answer to this—how much do you want to cut? Memory wire bracelets and rings can be one loop around your wrist or finger, multiple loops, or even less than one full loop—the choice is yours. However, when it comes to necklaces you'll find that it's much more comfortable to only wear a piece made with a single loop.

145 Cutting memory wire

As it's made from toughened steel, only special cutters will cut memory wire and live to tell the tale. When buying cutters, always check that they will work on this material as memory wire destroys unspecialized cutters.

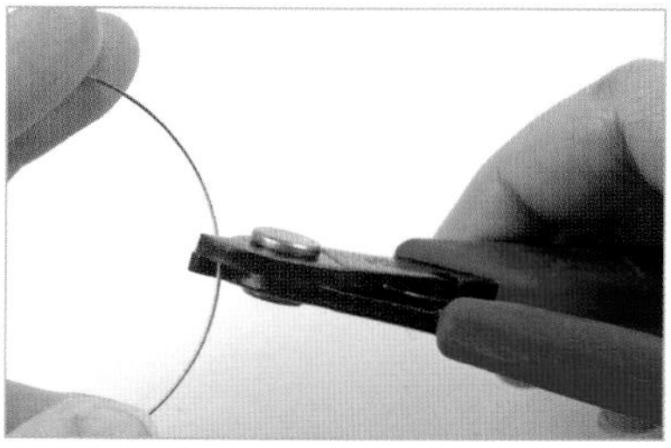

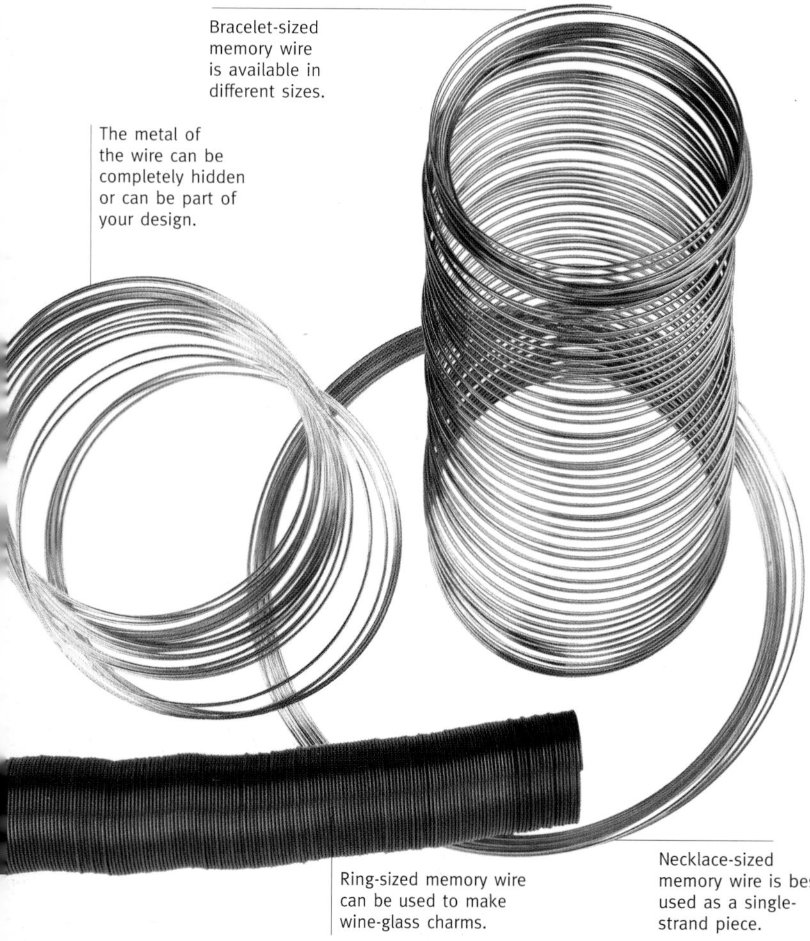

TRY IT

146 Beyond beads

When using memory wire, you can begin to think beyond beads and string items that may be likely to wear away at more fragile stringing materials. Because it is made of toughened steel, memory wire stands up to rubbing against metal so is ideal for hanging charms or for gemstones with jagged edges.

Bracelet-sized memory wire is available in different sizes.

The metal of the wire can be completely hidden or can be part of your design.

Ring-sized memory wire can be used to make wine-glass charms.

Necklace-sized memory wire is best used as a single-strand piece.

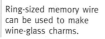

147

How to end it

There are two ways to finish your memory wire. Each has its own benefits, so make your choice according to your needs.

When making loops in your wire, ensure you bend the wire so the loops sit outside the bracelet and not inside where they might press into the wearer's wrist.

 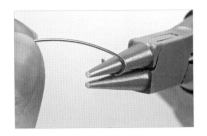

END BEADS

End beads not only stop your beads from falling off, they give a more decorative look to your piece, require more materials, and cost more.

1 Put a drop of glue in the hole in your end bead and place the end of your memory wire into it.

2 Leave to dry fully before stringing and then repeat at the other end.

TURNED LOOPS

A turned loop in your wire is quick and easy to do and is there to stop your beads from falling off the ends.

1 Using round-nose pliers, grasp the end of your wire and turn a loop until the cut end touches itself. You might not be able to turn a full loop in one go, so take as many steps as you need to get the right result.

2 Thread on your beads, making sure you leave enough wire, then finish the second end in the same way as the first.

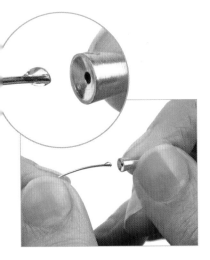

FIX IT

148 Losing your ends?

If you're having trouble getting your end beads to stay on your memory wire, then roughen the ends of the wire with a file or emery board to help the glue adhere before placing them in the beads.

149 Want a clasp?

Although memory wire doesn't need a clasp, some people like the security of having one on a piece of jewelry. This is not a problem—simply finish the wire using loops and use these to attach the clasp of your choice, or you can even buy memory wire ends with a loop, perfect for attaching a clasp.

SEE ALSO:

Crimping, page 52
Threads and knots,
page 56
Using cord and
ribbon, page 60
Turned loops,
page 74
Wrapped loops,
page 76

Multistrand vs illusion cord

String jewelry can be bold or discreet—you may wish to replicate great stringing material in multistrand pieces, or you might want the beads to take center stage and choose a more subtle material like illusion cord. It all depends on the beads.

150

Multistrand necklaces

Multiple strands dramatically alter the look of a necklace. You can make them using cords and ribbons—simply place more than one strand into your cord ending, thread, knot multiple pieces together and hide inside a calotte, or use more strands of flexible wire, cord, or thread, and hide the ends with an end cone. Here are some options.

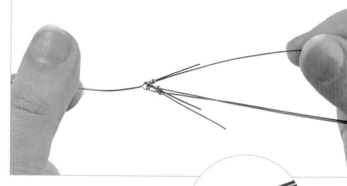

USING AN EYEPIN
You can crimp multiple pieces of wire onto an eyepin, thread this through your end cone, and finish using a turned or wrapped loop to secure the wire in place.

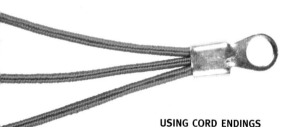

USING CORD ENDINGS
More than one piece of cord or ribbon will fit into a cord ending—a useful device for disguising frayed cord and thread, or poorly cut wire.

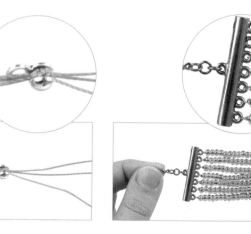

USING END CONES
Like cord endings, end cones are very useful for holding multiple strands together. They can also be used on single strand pieces to hide your finishing and add decoration.

USING A CALOTTE
Knotting multiple threads together and placing them inside a calotte is a simple and fast way to hide the join where the multiple threads meet.

SPACER BARS
Spacer bars can be used to keep different strands held together—ideal for chokers and bracelets.

GETTING YOUR STRANDS RIGHT

The trick to getting your multistrand piece right is to play around with the lengths of the different strands. Use a bead design board to help you work out lengths. As different techniques, beads, and bodies will make each finished piece lie differently, it's always best to test how they will actually look. Before securing the strands, test them on an EZ Sizer or jewelry bust, or model them yourself, to see if the different lengths work well together.

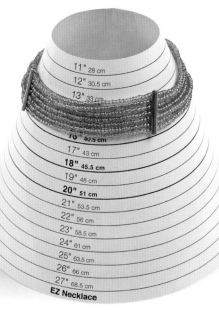

A jewelry bust is ideal when planning multistrand pieces as it reflects how the necklace will look when worn.

Play around with the space between individual strands for different looks.

Illusion and floating necklaces

This type of necklace is hugely popular and can be made in many different ways using a variety of techniques. The aim is to have just a few beads on the necklace to give the illusion that they are simply floating. The beads need to be secured so they don't move around and you can choose to crimp, knot, or glue to achieve this. You can also choose to have single or multiple strands, more or fewer beads, and a stringing material that is more or less invisible.

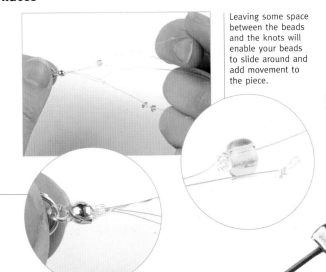

Leaving some space between the beads and the knots will enable your beads to slide around and add movement to the piece.

Crimps on flexible wire will stop your beads from moving around. However, you may find the crimps rough against your skin.

Multiple strands of illusion cord with knots, or dots of glue, can be finished with calottes.

Wirework

Wirework is a fun and quick way to express yourself in jewelry making. Although you're working in metal, you can bend and form these materials to achieve the look, shape, and feel you want. A few simple techniques are all that is needed to create some wonderful jewelry, as you will see in the following pages.

Wirework tips and tricks

Although wirework can be achieved with only a few materials, tools, and techniques, great wirework is dependent on knowing the tips, tricks, and trade secrets that will help you achieve a professional finish.

SEE ALSO:

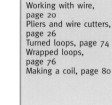

Working with wire, page 20
Pliers and wire cutters, page 26
Turned loops, page 74
Wrapped loops, page 76
Making a coil, page 80

152 Wire forming

The most important tip in wirework is to notice that often it's not actually your tools that form and shape your wire—it's your fingers. You simply use the pliers as a form to bend the wire around. If you examine the picture on the left, you'll see that, although it looks like the pliers are making the loop, it's actually the thumb pressing the wire onto the pliers that's doing the work.

153 Unmarked wire

When you first start wirework, you might find that you're marking your wire. Don't worry—the main cause of this is gripping the wire too tight while you're learning how to control it. Once you have some more practice and relax, you'll find this happens a lot less. If it still occurs, you can wrap masking tape around the jaws of your pliers to soften them.

154 Get in close

Always hold your work as close to the action as you can. You will have much better control over it. If you look at the photos, you can see in the one on the left that there's a much greater chance of the wire bending in the wrong place, than in the one on the right.

155 Perfect sized loops

There are a number of tricks to getting the same-sized loops using a pair of regular round-nose pliers.

USING THE BASE OF YOUR PLIERS
Always use the base of your pliers to make your loops. This method is the easiest to follow and ensures your loops are the same size. The down side is they may be larger than you'd like.

MARKING YOUR PLIERS
You can mark your pliers either with a permanent marker or on a piece of masking tape stuck onto the jaw of your pliers.

USING A PREVIOUS LOOP AS A GUIDE
Thread a previous loop onto the jaw of your pliers and note where it sits. Use this as a guide of where to make your next loop.

156 Hold it steady

Whenever you need to hold and grip wire, make sure you use a pair of pliers with a flat inner jaw. This means that any pressure you put on the wire is spread out and is a lot less likely to mark your wire. Holding wire with round-nose pliers focuses all the pressure into a smaller point and adds unwanted dents and grooves.

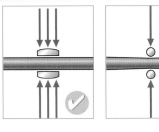

157 Out of reach

When working with lots of pairs of pliers, it's all too easy to think you're picking up your flat-nose and oops they were your wire cutters, and disaster has struck. Always aim to put your wire cutters out of easy reach so you never pick them up without intending to.

158 Keep it real

When practicing, always use a colored wire such as copper. Not only it is a lot more affordable, but it also makes it easier to tell your scrap metal from your real sterling silver wire. You might also find that you prefer the look of the cheaper wire.

159 Hands off

When working with your wire it is often tempting to be lazy and hold your wire with your hands instead of a pair of pliers. Resist the temptation! You will not get as good a grip on your wire and subsequently not as neat a finish. Persevere with using two pairs of pliers until it becomes second nature and the results will be worth it.

160 Don't worry

As you make your loops and components, you'll be examining your work up close and you'll be able to spot minute differences. But when these loops and components are part of a finished piece, the difference won't be noticeable. This is especially true of loops that are joined to each other.

Imperfect shapes and rough textures add character to your jewelry—running after perfection all the time is not necessarily the best move.

These loops are differently sized and not completely round, which is obvious when they're examined up close.

But as soon as the loops are joined together, you won't notice any difference.

SEE ALSO:

Working with wire,
page 20
Pliers and wire cutters,
page 26
Wirework tips and
tricks, page 70

Cutting and filing wire

The first skill to learn when you want to work with wire is how to cut and file it. A few tips and tricks will help you do so safely and ensure you get the result you want.

Choosing your cutters

The two common forms of wire cutters are side or end cutters, each of which are used in the same way. As side cutters are the most commonly available and useful, these are used throughout this book.

Side cutters will enable you to get in closer to your work.

Cutting the wire

Before you ever cut a piece of wire, take a look at your wire cutters. You'll notice that there are two sides to the blade. One is flat and the other is slanted where the blades meet. Always cut your wire with the flat side facing your work as you are able to get closer in. Using the other side will leave a length of wire that sits in the slanted space before it meets the blade.

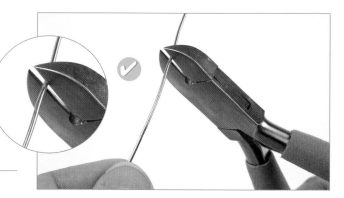

Cutting with the flat side facing your work will enable you to get as close as possible to the desired length.

Cutting wire economically

The best tip for saving wire is to cut more! Put simply, if you estimate that you need 3½in (9cm) of wire, don't cut 4in (10cm)—cut at least 8in (20cm) as this will leave you with a long enough length to be useful. Scraps of tiny lengths of wire are no good, but keep anything longer in a pot and use it next time you just need a small piece of wire.

End cutters can handle thicker wire but you may find it tricky to get in close.

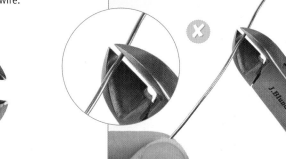

Cutting with the slanted side facing your work will result with a length of wire sticking out uncut from your work.

164

Filing your wire

After cutting your wire, you may need to file the ends to remove any sharp burrs and to give a smoother finish that won't catch on your skin. This is especially important when making an earring finding.

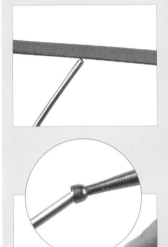

METAL FILES
Specially designed metal files can be purchased. These come in a variety of tooth configurations that will help you remove any sharp edges.

EMERY BOARDS
An emery board can also be used to remove any burrs and sharp points. However, it won't be suitable for filing large amounts.

CUP BURRS
Cup burrs (or burr cups) are ideal for rounding the end of your wire. These can also be placed in an electric drill if you plan on filing a lot of ends at one time.

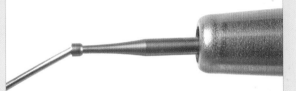

WIRE ROUNDERS
Wire rounders are cup burrs with a wooden handle which makes them easier to grip.

165

Safety in mind

When cutting wire, always keep safety in mind.
• Keep your fingers and thumbs away from the cutting blade at all times.
• Keep fingers and other parts of your hand away from the hinges.
• Try and hold both the wire you want to keep and the wire you're removing, so that it doesn't fly off.
• Point your wire down and away from you. This means that if the wire does fly off, it's less likely to fly toward you or anyone else.

Holding onto the wire you're cutting off will ensure it doesn't fly off and injure anyone.

166

Cutting chain

Chain is a functional and decorative component in jewelry making but it can be awkward to count and cut equal lengths when required. The trick to this is to cut one piece the length you require, and thread this onto a piece of wire or headpin alongside the next piece of chain to be cut. When the chains hang down, it will be easier to cut them to the same length.

Turned loops

Turned loops are the most basic wirework technique and probably the most useful. They enable you to make earrings, bracelets, and necklaces, turn simple shapes into charms and dangles, and join components together. There are two methods to making a turned loop, both of which are described here, and both of which are easy to master.

SEE ALSO:

Working with wire, page 20
Essential findings, page 40
Wirework tips and tricks, page 70
Cutting and filing wire, page 72
Opening and closing loops, page 82

167

Turned loop on a piece of wire

This method of making a loop is the easiest, but it only works when you don't have a bead on the wire and when you're making the first loop of a component.

1 Grasp the end of a piece of wire with your round-nose pliers. Make sure you grasp the very end of the wire, as any left sticking out will not bend into your loop.

2 Turn the pliers, either toward or away from you, to begin turning your loop—choose whichever feels more comfortable. Note that to get the best result you need to work with your fingers close to the loop. Also note that it is actually your thumb forming the loop around the pliers rather than the pliers doing the work.

3 You will have to reposition the pliers to finish the loop rather than try to complete it in one movement. As soon as it feels uncomfortable, take your pliers out, adjust your hand, place the pliers back in, and continue turning until the wire touches itself.

4 You now have a "P" shape that you need to centralize so it sits straight above the rest of the wire. Put one of the points of your round-nose pliers into the loop you made and the other resting where the wire touches itself. Use the pliers and your thumb to bend the wire and form more of a "lollipop" shape.

5 To finish, you need to adjust the loop, and possibly close it up if it has opened at all when finishing. It is always best to do this after you have looked at it with a bead threaded on, as it will look very different. You can do this adjusting with your round- or flat-nose pliers or fingers. Adding the bend may also have made the loop open slightly, so close it now.

168 Turned loop with a bead

If you're going to make another loop at the other end of your wire, or on a head- or eyepin with a bead, the technique is slightly different, as you'll now have a bead in the way.

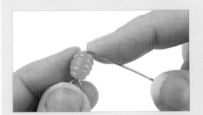

1 Thread a bead onto the other end of your wire, or your head- or eyepin. Make sure you hold the bead firmly against the bottom of the pin or the loop so you don't leave any space. Bend the wire against the top of the bead so that it now lies at a 90-degree angle to the bead.

2 Trim the wire—there is no easy way to know exactly how much wire to leave as everyone makes different-sized loops. Remember, you can always trim more off but you can't put wire back on. To start with, try leaving around ½in (1cm).

3 You now need to turn the wire back on itself above the bend you made. Hold the wire so the cut end is pointing away from you and turn your hand away from you so that your palm is facing upward. Grasp the end and turn the pliers toward you, stop when it becomes uncomfortable, reposition your hand and pliers, and then continue until the wire touches itself and the loop is made. Once you've finished the loop, you can adjust it as you did the first one.

169 Losing the loop

As you turn, you want to make sure you aren't losing the bend you made. To do this, make sure you're only turning the end of the wire into a loop and not pulling all of the wire around.

FIX IT

170 One smaller loop

If you have cut too much wire and your second loop is larger than the first, you can simply "undo" the larger loop using your round-nose pliers and trim a tiny amount of wire away and re-turn.

171 Large bead hole

If you want to use a bead that has such a large hole that the headpin slips through it, don't worry, you can still use the bead, but thread a smaller bead on the pin first to hold it in place.

Thread a bead onto a headpin, make a loop, attach a finding, and voila! New earrings!

Chains made up of beads joined by turned loops are easy to make and look great.

Wrapped loops

Wrapped loops are not only decorative but also practical. Perfect for adding security to your work, they also add decoration and can be used to alter the look of a piece by increasing the amount of wire on display. This technique can be more complicated to learn, especially as you use two different types of pliers at one time, but with practice, you'll soon be turning out professional wrapped loops.

SEE ALSO:

Beginning with beads, page 10
Essential findings, page 40
Wirework tips and tricks, page 70
Turned loops, page 74

172

Making a wrapped loop

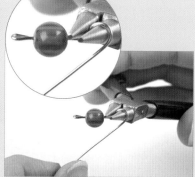

1 Thread your bead onto a head- or eyepin. You need to ensure you have at least 1½in. (4cm) of wire left at the top of the bead. Press the bead tight against the end of the pin and hold the wire above it with your flat- or chain-nose pliers. Press the wire against the tool using your finger or thumb to bend the wire over at a right angle. The space between the bead and the bend is where your wraps will sit, so how much space you leave is your choice. If you want fewer wraps, leave less space.

2 Grasp the wire at the bend with your round-nose pliers, and then bend the length of wire around your pliers to form a loop.

3 Bring the wire right around until it crosses over itself. Note that as you do this, the wire will hit the pliers and you will need to turn your pliers out of the way to finish the loop.

If your wire hits the pliers, your work will be a mess.

Rotate your pliers so the jaws are out of the way and the wire doesn't hit them.

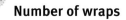

173 Straight wraps

The tip to getting your wraps nice and straight is to ensure that, when you make your loop, the wire crosses over itself at right angles and doesn't bend up or down.

174 Number of wraps

The length of wire left at the top of the bead, between the bead and before the bend, is the area that will be covered by your wire wraps. The ideal amount of wraps is between one and five—any more than that and it can get unwieldy and the whole piece begins to distort.

175 Joining wrapped loops

Unlike turned loops, once a wrapped loop is made it can no longer be opened. This means that you have to remember to join one to another at the right stage. When you have made the loop on your second piece, and crossed the wire over, thread this through your first loop and wrap to finish.

4 There are two ways to hold the piece now to finish. You can either hold the round-nose pliers in your non-dominant hand with the points facing upward and the loop you have made placed over one of the jaws (as in step 3). Alternatively, you can place the loop between the jaws of a pair of flat-nose pliers, as shown below.

5 Grip the end of your wire with a pair of flat- or chain-nose pliers and begin to wrap it around the small section of wire that sits above the bead, after the loop. The best way to do this is to pull the wire around in a large circle, going slowly to make sure the wraps sit neatly next to each other and moving down toward the bead.

7 When you reach your bead, trim the wire as close as you can, and then press in the end so it doesn't catch on your skin.

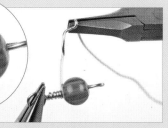

6 Stop wrapping when you reach your bead, or continue wrapping to add a decorative wirework cap (see page 78).

ALTERNATIVE METHOD
To get a neater finish you can use crimping pliers. Place the end notch over the cut end and press gently—you will find that the cut end is pushed in and rounded into your work.

176

Wrapped bead

1 When wrapping, you don't have to stop once you meet the bead. Continue on to cover the bead and you have your own decorative bead cap or decorated pendant drop.

2 To finish, trim your wire and turn a simple loop at the end of the wire. Press this end in close to your bead to add a decorative look to what would otherwise be just the cut end of wire.

Adding a wrapped cap to a bead creates a pretty look that frames the bead's shape.

177

Even loops

Always make sure you keep your loop as far down the pliers as they will go. If the loop is able to wobble about, like the one in the photo on the right, it will become distorted.

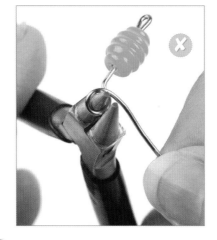

FIX IT

179 Forgot to join your loops?

It is very easy to be so focused on wrapping that you forget to join your loops. Don't despair—they can always be joined afterward with jump or split rings.

178

Double-ended wrap

Rather than thread your bead onto a head- or eyepin you can make a wrapped loop at both ends. Begin with a length of wire and, near the center, make a right-angled bend. This is where you'll make your loop and begin to wrap the wire around itself. As you haven't yet set a space, you can add as many wraps as you choose at this end. Continue to finish the wrapped loop, thread on a bead, and make another wrap at the second end.

For a double-ended wrap, begin by forming a wrapped loop at one end, thread on a bead (if you like), and then make another wrap to complete.

180 Wrapped drop

Pendant and drop beads are easy to combine with wrapped loops to create lovely earrings, pendants, or charms. As this will only ever be a dangle and not a component part of a piece, it doesn't need the security or strength of a true wrapped loop.

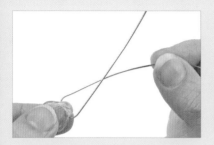

1 Place a length of wire through your bead. Bend both pieces of wire so that they cross over the top of the bead. Make sure the wires cross centrally above your bead.

2 Use flat- or chain-nose pliers to bend one of the wires so that it points straight up, with the bend centrally placed on top of the bead. Bend the other end so it lays out to one side. Make sure the bead can still move freely so it isn't in danger of cracking.

3 Use your pliers to hold the bead, where the wires cross, in your non-dominant hand, and begin to wrap the horizontal wire around the piece that's sticking straight up.

4 When you've made as many wraps as you want, finish, trim the piece of wire used to wrap, and neaten the cut end.

5 Use the remaining wire to make a turned loop to finish.

Wrapped drops can be used as pendants or earrings. The technique explained above ensures the beads hang well and aren't damaged.

FIX IT

181 Get closer to the bead

If you find that you are unable to get your wire close to the bead without the risk of it cracking, then use a finer wire. This will enable you to make a neater-looking wrapped drop with less space between the wire and the bead.

182 Handling fragile beads

Unlike most other beads with holes going through their widest central part, drop beads have their holes to one side, surrounded by a thinner area of glass. This means that they're much more likely to crack and break. To prevent this, always ensure that, as you make the wrapped drop, the bead can move freely. As soon as it can't move, you know it's held too tightly and is in danger of cracking.

Making a coil

Coils are great if you want to add decoration and shape using a simple, versatile technique. Once you've mastered the steps, learn how you can play around with their shape and size, and even discover how to turn a simple piece of wire into your own designer earrings.

SEE ALSO:

Working with wire, page 20
Using memory wire, page 64
Cutting and filing wire, page 72
Turned loops, page 74
Adding texture, page 84

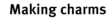

183

Making a coil

Coils can be varied by adjusting how many times you wind the wire around, the size of the central hole, and even how neatly you work. But in each case the basic method stays the same.

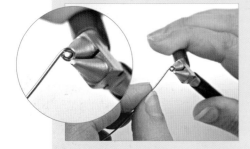

1 Cut a 4in (10cm) piece of wire. Using the tip of your round-nose pliers, make a loop and stop when the wire touches itself.

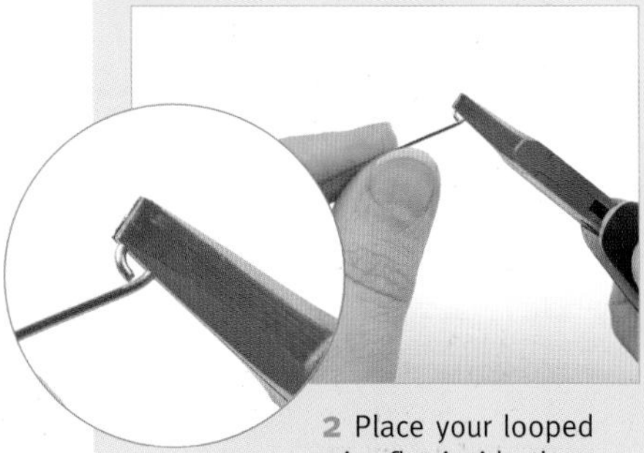

2 Place your looped wire flat inside the jaws of a pair of flat-nose pliers. You need to make sure the tail of the wire curves away from you.

3 Hold your pliers firmly in one hand and press the thumb of the other hand against the wire right up at the loop. Continue pressing with your thumb and rotate your other hand away from you.

4 Continue pressing with one hand while rotating the other and your coil will soon start to form.

5 Stop when you're happy with the size of your coil.

184

Making charms

A few simple bends and your plain flat coils are turned into dangles and embellishments perfect for stringing and adorning your jewelry.

1 Using a pair of flat-nose pliers, bend your remaining straight wire away from your coil.

2 Use round-nose pliers to make a turned loop and create your charm.

You could add a bead before you make your turned loop, for more decorative dangles.

185 Making earrings

A few extra turns and you've made your own wirework earrings.

1 After making your coil and bending the wire away from it, place a pair of round-nose pliers a short distance away from the coil and bend the wire around the jaws. The distance you make this bend from the coil will determine how low the earrings hang.

2 Trim and file the ends of the wire.

3 Using flat-nose pliers, add a kink to the wire so the earrings don't work their way out when worn.

187 Making a neat coil

To get a neat result with all the coils touching each other, you need to make sure you keep your thumb close to your work where each curve is being made. Pressing your thumb further away than this can result in a messy coil, with each new curve not matching the previous one.

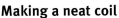

FIX IT

188 Making pairs

If you want to make matching pairs of coils, the key is to match them up every step of the way. Start by cutting all the pieces of wire the same length. Then make all the loops, turn all the coils, and make all the final bends. This way you can easily compare each piece, rather than trying to match them up at the end.

186 Varying the coils

There are lots of different ways you can vary and play around with these coils:

• Try making smaller and larger central holes by using different parts of your round-nose pliers to form the first loop.

• Make more or fewer rotations to change the finished size.

• Start to become more random and less neat, and your coils will develop spaces and begin to change shape.

• Finish your coil by forming the wire around your round-nose pliers to add a flowery look.

• Apply the hammer to add texture.

SEE ALSO:

Pliers and wire cutters,
page 26
Essential findings,
page 40
Turned loops, page 74

Opening and closing loops

When making jewelry and playing with wirework, you'll come across all sorts of loops that need opening and closing. Although they may look different, and be used in different ways, the same method is used to open and close them securely and neatly.

189

Opening and closing jump rings

This method applies whether you're opening a jump ring, the attaching loop on an earring finding, the loop on a calotte, or a turned loop you have made. The only difference will be whether you use one or two pairs of pliers.

1 Hold your jump ring with two pairs of pliers, one each side of the cut in the ring. You'll find it easier to control your work if you hold the pliers across as much of the ring as you can (shown correctly below).

Try not to hold your jump rings with the tips of your pliers as this gives you less grip and will mean you have to use more strength to open the ring.

2 Pull your dominant hand toward you. Doing it this way makes it easier for you to link rings and components together. You want to open the ring enough to be able to thread on any other item.

3 Once you've joined the required components, reverse the previous step and push your dominant hand forward. You now need to close any remaining gap and add more security to the closed ring. Push your dominant hand forward slightly, so that the ends of the ring are no longer level. Next, push your hands together slightly so that the ends of the ring cross each other as though you were squashing the ring.

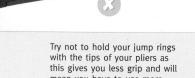

Once you get the hang of opening and closing loops, you won't be able to stop!

Opening other loops

Any other loop is opened using the same method, but you will need to hold one side of the loop in your hand and a pair of pliers in the other.

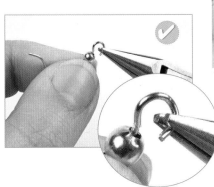

Never open a ring by unlooping it. This can weaken it as well as flatten the loop—it is a lot more work opening and closing it this way.

Using a central jump ring to hang your pendant from ensures it sits directly in the middle of your necklace.

Simple loops can be threaded onto a hoop earring for a mix and match look.

5 To finish, adjust the ring so that the ends meet together neatly. The previous steps will have "work hardened" the wire slightly so that when you bring the ends together, they will want to push past each other and there should be no gap.

4 Pull the ends back and repeat the previous step so that they cross each other in the opposite way.

FIX IT

191   **One end higher than the other?**

If one end sticks up above the other, push the ring between your pliers and press down to level them out.

Adding texture

Adding texture to your wirework is not only a great design feature, but it is also fun to do. Texture changes the look of a piece, adds interest, and ensures it catches the light as well as giving a finished look to the work.

SEE ALSO:

Pliers and wire cutters, page 26
Turned loops, page 74
Wrapped loops, page 76
Making a coil, page 80

192 The tools and set-up

The main tools you will need are a hammer and a steel block. Also useful is a thick towel, which is folded and placed underneath the block to lessen the noise and to protect your work surface. You can also place the block and towel on the floor to protect your work surface.

193 Be creative with your hammer

The rounded end of your hammer is perfect for adding all those dents and kinks to your work, which give it texture and catch the light. Simply hammer your work until you have added as much texture as you require.

A hammered coil adds texture and interest.

HAMMERING WITH BEADS ON

Always try to hammer your work before you put any beads on. Beads act as a magnet to your hammer and may end up smashed. If you have to have a bead there, you can try to protect it by placing a wallpaper scraper or metal ruler alongside it. This helps to guide the hammer down and away from the bead as you hammer.

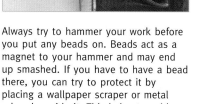

You may prefer different looks depending on what you're making. Experiment by making samples and seeing which best suits your current piece.

HAMMERING IN THE RIGHT PLACES

When hammering a piece that you will want to later thread a bead onto, you need to be careful not to hammer it so much that it widens and will no longer fit the hole of your bead.

SAFETY FIRST

Always make safety a priority when using a hammer and block as it is all too easy to get fingers in the way and end up hurting yourself. The main trick is to leave a handle on the piece you want to hammer so that you can hold your work while keeping your hand a safe distance from danger.

FLATTENING

You can flatten your work without adding dents by using the flat side of your hammer. Being careful and not catching your work with the edges of your hammer will give you an attractive, flattened look.

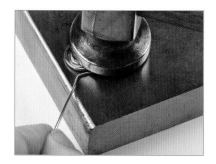

Making wire findings

One of the best ways to explore wirework
is by making and designing your own findings.
Earring findings are quick and easy to make
and infinitely variable.

SEE ALSO:

Essential findings,
page 40
Making a coil, page 80

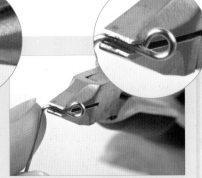

194

Making your own earring findings

When you begin to examine findings
and other wire items, you will soon
notice that a lot of them can be
easily replicated.

1 Cut a 1½in (4cm) piece of wire. Using
the points of your round-nose pliers,
make a small turned loop at one end.

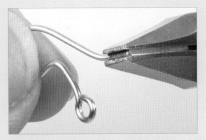

2 Hold the wire above the loop with
your flat-nose pliers and make a right-
angled bend in the wire.

3 Use the base of your round-nose
pliers, or the largest step of your
three-step pliers, to make a fairly
large loop.

4 Trim your wire and file the end so
it doesn't cut you. Make a kink in the
wire so it doesn't easily come out of
your ear.

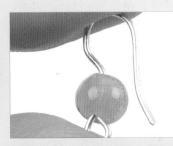

5 The finished finding. Try decorating
the finding with a single bead by
threading it on before you make
your bend.

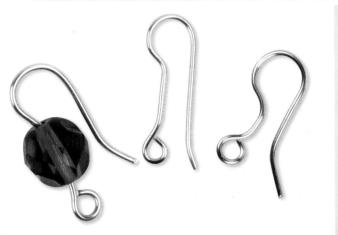

TRY IT

195 **Combining techniques**

All wirework techniques are ideal for combining and
creating your own designs. Looking for inspiration?
Look at jewelry-making books and websites,
browse finished jewelry in stores, and check out
what others are wearing—but most importantly,
sit and play with your wire and beads.

Beadweaving

Beadweaving with small seed beads can seem a daunting world at first, filled with technical terms, strange bead sizes and weights, and lots of new materials. The following pages will clear up all the confusion and teach you the techniques, terms, and tricks you will need to get beading. You will learn how to bead and identify the different beading stitches, discover all those thread and tension tips that will take your work to a new level, and find out how to change a stitch from flat to circular or tubular. You will also explore which stitch is best for what you want to create, learn how to follow patterns and charts, and discover the difference between loom work and off-loom beadweaving.

SEE ALSO:

Quick tips and tricks, page 91

Working with thread

The main material you will use in beadweaving is, of course, thread. The type and length of thread you use is your choice, but there are many thread-related tips and tricks to help you along the way.

196

Threading your needle

One of the hardest tricks to learn when beginning beading is how to thread those small-eyed needles.

Making sure the end of your thread has a sharp, clean cut will help you to thread your needle.

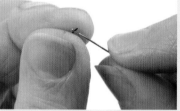

1 Bringing your thread to the eye of your needle is a difficult method to use as it gives the thread a chance to slip around either side of the needle rather than go through the eye. The trick is to bring the needle to the thread instead.

2 Hold your thread with the sharply cut end sitting between your thumb and index finger on your non-dominant hand—you want to hold it so you can barely see it. The more you can see of it, the more it is able to move and the harder it will be to thread.

3 Bring the eye of your needle down to the thread and push it onto it. This gives the thread the only option of going through the eye. As soon as a piece of the thread is through you can continue pushing or pull the rest of the thread through.

FIX IT

197 **Stretching your thread**

When your thread comes off the reel it will be still coiled, making it much more likely to tangle together and get knotted. The cure for this is to stretch it. Pull your thread with your hands with sufficient force to straighten it. You'll find it is now a lot easier to work with.

FIX IT

198 **Can't thread your needle?**

Because of how needles are made, the eye on one side of your needle will be slightly larger than on the other. Try both sides if you're having trouble threading it.

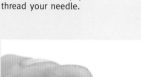

199 What is a workable length of thread?

Exactly what a workable length of thread is will vary from person to person, project to project, and technique to technique. Some people prefer a longer thread and some people prefer a short thread. An ideal length to work with is your arm span, which is the distance from your right-hand index finger to your left-hand index finger. Try this length and then see if you're happy with it or would prefer a shorter or longer length. Do remember you need to leave thread at the start of your work to help you finish your work later. To help you make your decision, the pros and cons are laid out below.

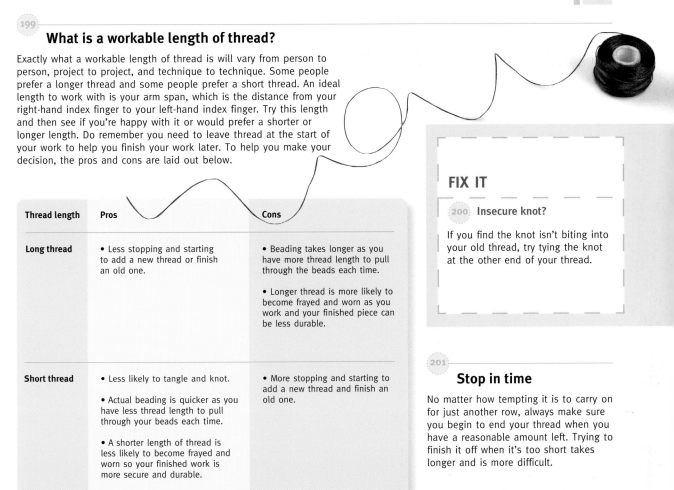

Thread length	Pros	Cons
Long thread	• Less stopping and starting to add a new thread or finish an old one.	• Beading takes longer as you have more thread length to pull through the beads each time. • Longer thread is more likely to become frayed and worn as you work and your finished piece can be less durable.
Short thread	• Less likely to tangle and knot. • Actual beading is quicker as you have less thread length to pull through your beads each time. • A shorter length of thread is less likely to become frayed and worn so your finished work is more secure and durable.	• More stopping and starting to add a new thread and finish an old one.

FIX IT

200 Insecure knot?

If you find the knot isn't biting into your old thread, try tying the knot at the other end of your thread.

201 Stop in time

No matter how tempting it is to carry on for just another row, always make sure you begin to end your thread when you have a reasonable amount left. Trying to finish it off when it's too short takes longer and is more difficult.

202 Adding and finishing threads

Every beader will find their own method of joining in and finishing off threads and this can change from project to project. The most commonly used method to join in new threads is to weave the old one into your work to secure it, then weave in the new one and continue beading. This can be difficult at first, but the following diagram and pointers will help you join and finish your threads successfully.

ARE THE ENDS SECURE?
You need to ensure you have woven the ends in securely so they won't work their way out again. The best way to do this is to weave the thread over itself at least once—this will stop it pulling out so easily.

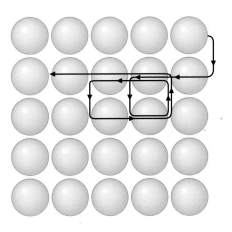

Weaving your thread over itself like this means it won't pull out easily when you don't want it to.

KEEP YOUR PLACE
If you weave away your old thread and then begin to weave in a new one, it can be hard to be sure where you last finished beading. To make sure this doesn't happen, always weave in your new thread before you trim the old thread to hold your place.

BEAD HOLES TOO FULL?
If you find your bead holes are too full to work out your old thread, don't worry. Begin beading again and once you have enough of a new section done, the holes of these beads will be less full and you can weave your thread through.

203
Making a slip knot

A quick method for adding and finishing threads is to deal with them both at once. This method won't work with beads with very small holes, or in a stitch where you thread the beads many times, as you will be working with three thicknesses. It works best if you use the end of the thread that comes off the reel first— you may find it easier to keep track of this by not cutting your new thread until you have joined it to the old one.

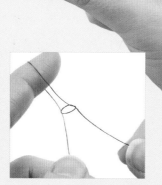

1 Make a loop near the end of your thread with the long length lying on top.

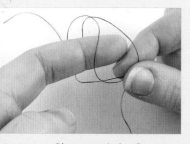

2 Place your index fingers through the thread loop and, taking hold of the long length of thread, pull it through the loop.

3 You will be left with a loop that you can adjust or loosen depending on which thread end you pull.

4 Place the end of your old thread end through the new loop and pull on the new thread to tighten the loop.

5 Ensure it has held by pulling on both threads to make sure they're tied together—if not, keep tightening the knot until they are. Continue beading and as you do so you will be weaving in both threads at once. If you want to add an extra level of security, you can weave through your previous work.

204
Thread tails

Visible thread tails can leave your work looking messy, so you will want to remove them as best you can. Use one of the two methods shown below.

TRIM THE TAILS
You can use a pair of sharp scissors to trim the thread tails as close to your work as possible.

BURN AWAY THREAD ENDS
Using a Thread Zap will enable you to get rid of any excess thread tails. But be careful not to burn away too much.

205
Plan ahead

You can ensure you don't have any thread ends left outside your work if you plan ahead slightly.

1 Before finishing, thread your needle into your work but stop before the eye enters it. Make sure you have threaded through a few beads.

2 Ensure the eye of your needle is close to your work and trim the thread so it is shorter than the length of the beads you have threaded through. Pull the needle all the way through and the thread end will disappear inside your work.

SEE ALSO:

Seed beads and
more, page 12
Working with thread,
page 88
Tension tips,
page 113

Quick tips and tricks

There are many tips, tricks, and short-cuts for working with seed beads and all of them will improve your work and practices. Explore all of those listed to see what works for you and if you can come up with any of your own.

206

The best beads to begin with

Start with the right beads for the project. Here are the points to consider:

Size: When you first start beadweaving, it's best to use a size you can easily see, e.g. size 8 or 11. Size 6 might be too big and make it hard to control the tension, whereas size 15 may be too small for you to see what you're doing.
Shape: You may find cylinder beads are good to begin with, as their flat sides mean the beads sit together evenly and enable you to see how your work is progressing more clearly.

The same is also true for bugle beads, but watch out for the sharp edges.
Finish: Using only shiny beads can be hard on your eyes and make it a lot harder for you to see what's going on so try to stick with matte beads at first.
Color: To help you to learn a new stitch and see exactly what you're doing, try using a different-colored bead for each row. This will aid you in seeing where you are up to and help you know what beads to thread through.

207

Using a stop bead

A stop bead is one threaded on at the start of your work to help with your tension as well as to stop your beads from falling off your thread. Simply pick up one bead, slide it toward the end of your thread, and circle back through it a few times, ensuring you don't split your thread. You need to thread through it enough times that it doesn't easily slide, but not so many that it will be hard to remove at the end of your work.

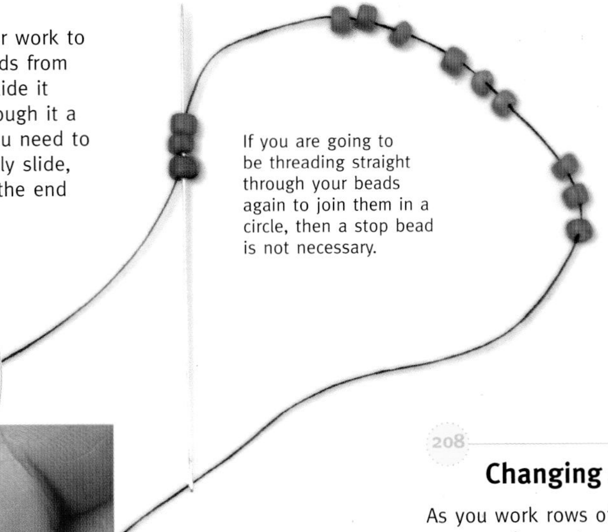

If you are going to be threading straight through your beads again to join them in a circle, then a stop bead is not necessary.

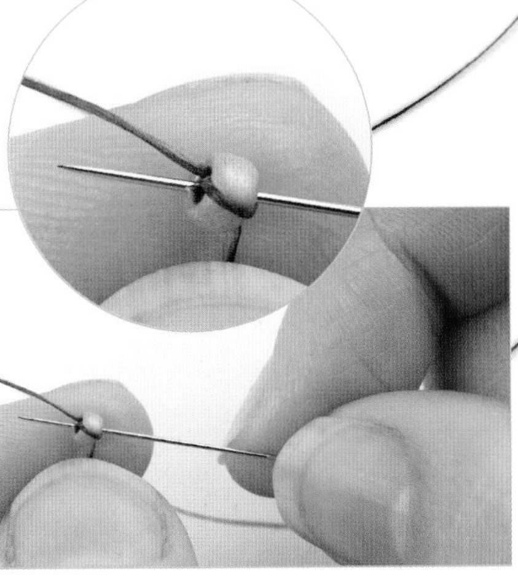

Thread through your stop bead so that it doesn't slide about.

208

Changing sides

As you work rows of beadwork, you can choose to either continually work in one direction—i.e. away from you or left to right, by turning your work around at the end of each row. Alternatively, you can choose not to turn your work but vary the direction with each row.

209

2-drop and beyond

2-drop, 3-drop, or 4-drop is a technique in which you use more than one bead in each space but treat them as if they were one bead. This means that every time you go to pick up or thread through a bead, you pick up or thread through two more. 2-drop is best explained using even- or odd-count peyote stitch (see page 105), as shown here.

1 Begin by picking up a number of pairs of beads. You will find it easier to see what you're doing at first if you pick up your pairs of beads in two different colors.

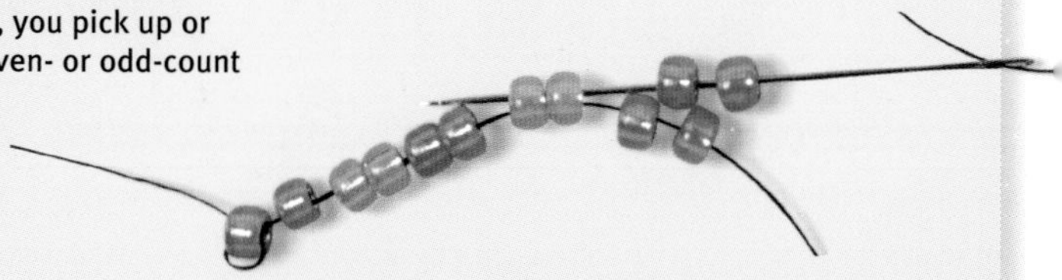

2 Pick up two beads in the same color as the last pair you added, and missing the last pair, thread back through the next. This means that pairs of beads of the same color will stack on top of one another.

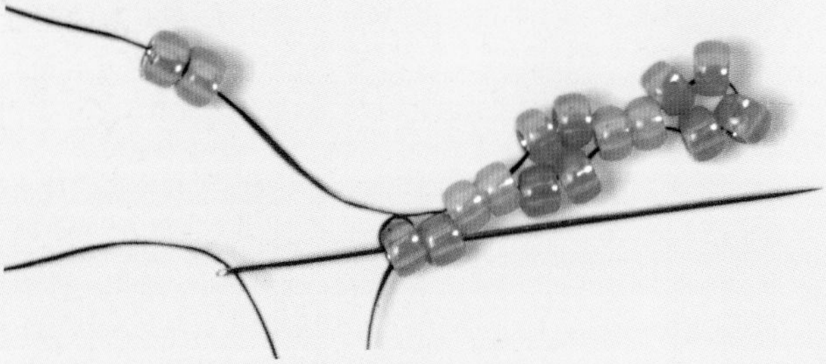

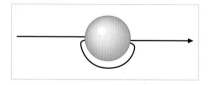

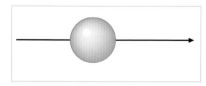

3 Continue adding pairs of beads and bead just as you would using regular peyote stitch. If it's odd-count peyote you're using, remember to perform your figure-eight turn at the end of the row (see page 107).

4 Two or more drop stitches can also be used to mix different bead sizes. This sample uses three seed beads treated as one, combined with bugle beads for a different look.

210

Circle through, go back through, and go through

All of these directions mean very different things, and understanding them can be the key to understanding a pattern or set of instructions.

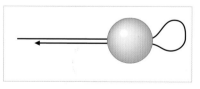

CIRCLE THROUGH
Circling through a bead means to go back through it in the same direction you previously threaded through it.

GO BACK THROUGH
To go back through a bead will require you to "go back" in the opposite direction to the original threading direction.

GO THROUGH
This technique does exactly what it says. If no other details are given, it can mean threading through a bead (usually a new one), or through the next bead along, in the same direction you have already been working.

211

Increasing

When increasing, keeping it gradual helps your work stay flat. This is the perfect opportunity to use those mis-sized beads. When increasing within your work, such as with peyote stitch, use two smaller-than-usual beads, which you then split in the next row. This will keep your increase more gradual and your work smoother. Alternatively, if you're after a more textured effect, add lots of extra beads and get your work ruffling!

212

Getting into position

With some seed bead stitches (e.g. peyote), when you add a new bead you will automatically be in the right position to continue, but with some (e.g. square, brick, herringbone, and ladder stitches as well as right-angle weave), you need to reposition your thread at each step to be in the right place to continue. Read through each beading stitch instruction to check the way to do this, as it varies for each one.

213

Thread for finishing

As soon as your working thread is only about 5in (12cm) long, stop using it and add a new one. Any thread length shorter than this may be more difficult to finish off neatly and cause you more hassle.

214

Read through

Always read through all beading instructions before you begin to ensure you have understood every step and have all the materials and tools you need before you get started.

FIX IT

215   Undoing your work and correcting a mistake

Never thread your needle back through your work as this makes it all too easy to split your thread and you will end up in a worse tangle than you were to begin with. Instead, remove your needle and gently undo the thread until you get back to where you made the mistake.

FIX IT

216   Stuck needle?

Sometimes you'll find that your needle gets stuck in your work. The first thing to assess is whether you'll be able to pull it out without cracking your bead. You may find that it helps to go backward as it will probably be the eye of the needle that's stuck. If it's still stuck, never be tempted to pull it through with your teeth, as you could injure yourself. Use something that will grip the needle better than your slippery fingers can. The following suggestions might help you:
• Pliers
• Piece of rubber (you can buy specially made tools or try a piece of rubber glove, rubber band, or balloon)
• Piece of cloth or tissue if that's all you have handy.

Pliers will grip a needle much better than your hands will.

A rubber glove will help you get a good grip on a stuck needle.

Ladder stitch

As well as being a stitch in its own right, ladder stitch is also the base for both brick and herringbone stitches. It is ideal for beginners as it is quick to bead, is comprised of only one row, and is easily embellished with fringes or loops as well as beads stitched over the top surface to add a whole new look. In ladder stitch, the individual beads, or group of beads in 2-, 3-, or 4-drop, are called rungs.

SEE ALSO:

Seed beads and more, page 12
Quick tips and tricks, page 91
Brick stitch, page 96
Herringbone stitch, page 100
Tension tips, page 113
Tubular beadwork, page 119

217

Designing with ladder stitch

Ladder stitch is only beaded as one row, which makes it easy for beginners. The threads go through each bead a few times, which makes it fairly durable. The following diagrams illustrate a few design possibilities.

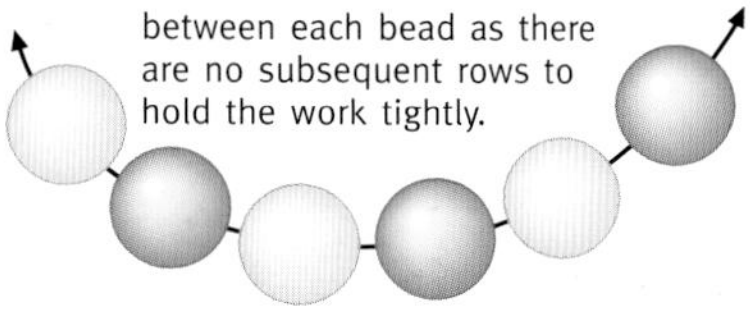

Ladder stitch can bend between each bead as there are no subsequent rows to hold the work tightly.

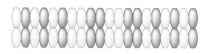

Stripes and blocks are easy to add to a piece of ladder stitch. Simply pick up your beads in alternate colors.

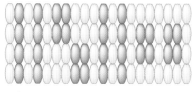

Beading 2-, 3-, or 4-drop ladder stitch gives you scope for adding patterns such as these.

218

Beading ladder stitch

Using bugle beads will help you to see what you are doing more clearly, but beware of sharp edges.

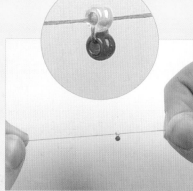

1 Thread your needle with a working length of thread. Pick up two beads and circle through the first one once again.

2 Pull the thread ends until the beads lie next to each other.

3 Circle through the second bead so you are in position to continue beading.

219

2-drop and beyond

Ladder stitch is ideal for experimenting with two or more beads to each stitch. Ensure that you treat the beads for each rung as if they were one bead.

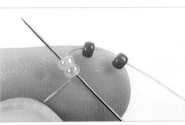

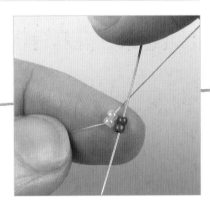

1 Begin by picking up double the amount of beads you want for each rung—if you are working 2-drop, then pick up four beads; if you are working 3-drop, pick up six beads.

2 Circle through the beads for the first rung.

3 Circle through the beads for the second rung to be in the correct position to continue.

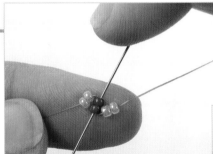

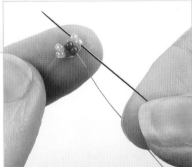

5 Repeat step 4 until your beadwork is the length you require.

4 Pick up the necessary beads for the next rung, circle through the previous rung to join them together, and then through the beads just picked up to be in the correct position to continue.

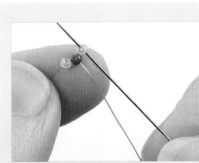

4 Pick up one new bead. Circle through the previous bead to join the new bead to it.

5 Circle through your new bead to be in the correct position to continue beading.

6 Repeat steps 4 and 5 to continue adding new beads until your work is the length you need.

Brick stitch

Brick stitch is named for its appearance—the beads sit in a brickwork-like pattern, which adds a design touch to the basic stitch. This stitch is ideal for beginners as it builds on a simple ladder stitch base—it becomes clear as you bead where the next bead needs to sit. Brick stitch is also known as "Comanche stitch," which derives from Native American beadwork.

SEE ALSO:

Quick tips and tricks, page 91
Ladder stitch, page 94
Peyote stitch, page 105
Tension tips, page 113
Tubular beadwork, page 119

220 Designing with brick stitch

The beads in a row of brick stitch sit flat beside each other but each row is offset from the one above, which gives the work its distinctive brickwork appearance. Note that the end beads of each row are offset so you won't achieve a straight line along them. Pieces of brick stitch are reasonably durable, but less so than other stitches as each row is joined to the one above only by linking threads, not by working through beads.

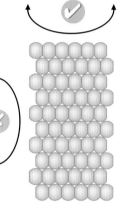

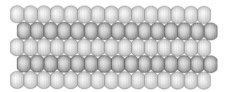

In brick stitch, you can bead stripes across the width. Simply pick up different-colored beads for each row you bead.

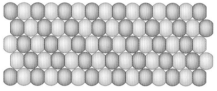

Diagonal stripes will work with brick stitch but straight stripes are often more eye-catching.

A piece of flat brick stitch will easily bend along its width, but not along its length.

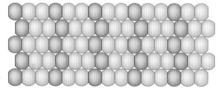

Stripes along the length will be zigzagged. If you want straight lines, use peyote stitch instead (see page 104). Just add different-colored beads to a row and then, in subsequent rows, place the same colored rows underneath them.

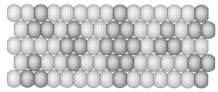

You can bead triangles and diamonds into your work as the beads sit offset from each other in each row.

221 Beading brick stitch

Brick stitch starts with a ladder stitch base and grows row by row from there. Each subsequent row is joined to the previous one bead-by-bead, and by loops under the threads which link the beads in the previous row. In brick stitch, each row can either have an in-bead start or an out-bead start and finish depending on what loop of thread you link to and how far along a row you bead. The different "starts" and "ends" are described on your right.

222 Two beads

You always begin a row of brick stitch by picking up two beads (see page 98). If you only picked up one bead, you would have a loop of thread showing at the start.

223 Ladder stitch increase

If you want to increase the edge of your beadwork by pairs of beads, you can use a ladder stitch increase to quickly do so. You can add as many pairs of beads as you require.

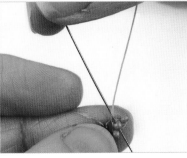
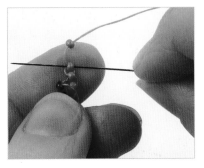

1 At the start or end of a row of ladder stitch, add a new bead onto the bead you're currently exiting.

2 Ladder stitch another bead to this new one and then use either an in- or out-bead start to begin a new row of brick stitch.

224 Shaping your work

You can use a combination of starts and ends to shape your work.

A wide ladder stitch base, with in-bead starts and ends in subsequent rows, will decrease both edges to form a triangle.

A narrow ladder stitch base with rows of out-bead starts and ends and then rows of in-bead starts and ends will form a diamond.

In-bead start
This begins a row with the first bead set in one space. The equivalent of decreasing at the start of a row.

In-bead end
The last bead of a row will sit in one space. The equivalent of decreasing at the end of a row.

Out-bead end
The last bead of a row will sit out one space. The equivalent of increasing at the end of a row.

Out-bead start
A row will start with the first bead sitting out one space. The equivalent of increasing at the start of a row.

Alternating in- and out-bead rows
If you want to keep your piece of beadwork with the same number of beads in each row and the sides as straight as possible, you need to bead alternate rows comprising an in-bead start and out-bead end with an out-bead start and an in-bead end.

In-bead ends

Out-bead starts
Out-bead ends
In-bead starts

225

In-bead starts

There are two different ways to bead an in-bead start to your row and which one you choose will depend on how secure you want your bead to be.

BASIC IN-BEAD START

1 Begin by beading a ladder stitch base the width you require for your piece. Pick up two seed beads and slide them down toward your work. Take your needle and thread under the loop of thread linking the second and third beads in your ladder.

2 Take your needle and thread back through the second bead just picked up and pull tight.

LOCKING STITCH FOR IN-BEAD START

You may find that the beads at the start of an in-bead row move around more than you'd like. If this is the case, you can add in a locking stitch that will hold them in place.

1 Begin as with a basic in-bead start by picking up two beads and linking under the loop of thread, linking the second and third beads in your ladder base.

2 Thread back through the first bead you picked up—not the second. Go back through the second bead again and under the thread loop again.

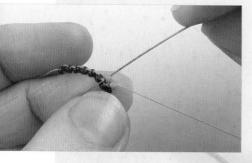

3 Take your needle and thread back through the second bead you picked up and pull tight.

226

Out-bead starts

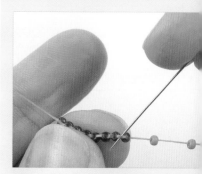

1 Pick up two beads and slide them down to your work. Thread under the first loop of thread, joining the first two beads in your previous row.

227

Continuing brick stitch

The remainder of the row in brick stitch is beaded using two simple steps.

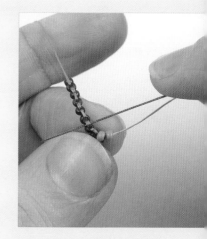

1 Pick up a third bead and slide it down to your work. Take your needle and thread under the next thread loop joining the beads in your ladder stitch base. Pull the thread so no slack remains.

BASIC OUT-BEAD START

This can be beaded straight onto a ladder stitch base or onto the first row of brick stitch to keep the row lengths even.

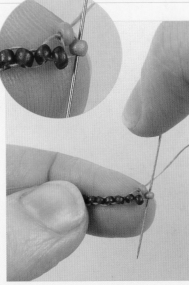

2 Thread back down the second bead just picked up and pull your thread tight.

LOCKING STITCH FOR OUT-BEAD START

Just as with an in-bead start, you may find that the beads at the start of your row move around more than you'd like. Try beading a locking stitch.

Begin, as with a basic out-bead start, by picking up two beads and linking under the loop of thread linking the first and second beads in your ladder. This time, thread back through the first bead just picked up, then through the second bead, link under your thread loop again, and then back through the second bead so that you are in position to continue beading your row.

2 Thread back through the bead just added and pull your thread tight so the bead lies nicely beside the ones already there. Repeat steps 1 and 2 to continue beading along the row.

228

Finishing your rows

You can choose to end your rows using either an in- or out-bead end.

IN-BEAD END

This means only beading to the last thread loop of the previous row or the ladder stitch base.

OUT-BEAD END

This involves adding two beads to the last thread loop of the previous row or the ladder stitch base.

Simply bead your row of brick stitch but stop once you have added a bead to the last thread loop.

1 Bead your row by adding a bead to each thread loop of the previous row or ladder stitch base.

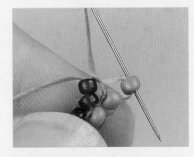

2 Pick up another bead and link this to the same end loop as you linked your previous bead. Thread back through this new bead to finish.

Herringbone stitch

Herringbone stitch is a decorative stitch in which the beads are added in pairs and lie in a herringbone pattern, which gives the stitch its name. It is also called "Ndebele" as it is used by the Ndebele people in South Africa. Although it is similar to brick stitch, it is more complicated and ideal for the more adventurous beader.

SEE ALSO:

Quick tips and tricks, page 91
Ladder stitch, page 94
Brick stitch, page 96
Tubular beadwork, page 119

229

Designing with herringbone stitch

The beads in a row of herringbone stitch sit slanted sideways, facing alternate ways, but each row sits flat on top of the previous one.

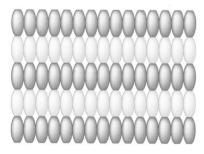

With herringbone stitch you can bead stripes along the width. Use a different color for each row you bead.

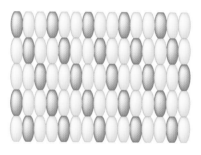

Diagonal stripes will work but they will be staggered due to how the beads lie in the final work.

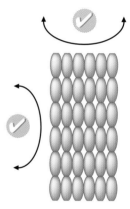

A piece of herringbone stitch will bend along its length and along its width.

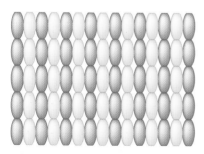

Stripes can be beaded along the length. Bead this by picking up the first of each pair of beads in one color and the second in another.

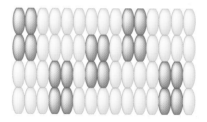

Blocks can be beaded into your designs. Simply pick up a pair of beads in one color and do the same with the pair you add on top of them.

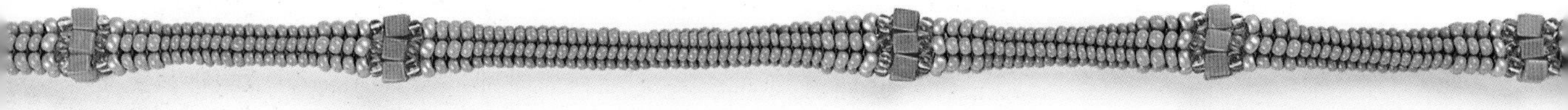

230

Beading herringbone stitch

Herringbone stitch is beaded in a similar way to brick stitch in that it begins with a ladder stitch base and each row is beaded from one side to the other. However, this time you add two beads at a time all the way along, and instead of just attaching to threads in the previous row, you work right through the beads of the previous row. As herringbone stitch is beaded with pairs of beads, your ladder stitch base must have an even number of beads in it.

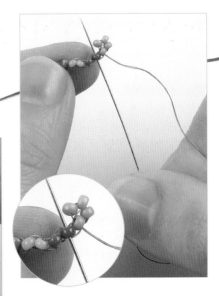

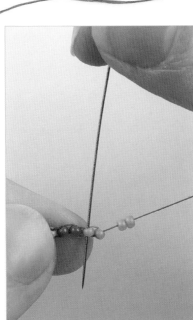

1 Begin with a ladder stitch base as wide as you want your piece of beadwork to be. This forms your first row. To help you work the stitch, at first you may find it easier to add your pairs of beads in different colors.

2 Pick up two beads that match the color of the bead you are already exiting; these are the first beads of your second row. Slide the beads down to your work and take your needle and thread down the second to end bead in your base row. This joins your new beads to the previous row.

3 Bring your needle and thread up through the third bead along in your base row and pull your thread tight to line up the new beads. This brings you back to the correct position to continue beading. Your beads should lie at a slant so that they form the distinctive herringbone pattern. If they don't automatically do this, you can use your fingernail or needle to adjust them.

231

Continuing herringbone stitch

Once you have beaded your ladder stitch base, herringbone stitch is easy to bead by repeating the same steps again and again until your work is the length you require.

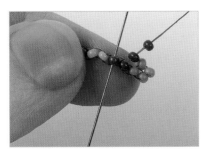

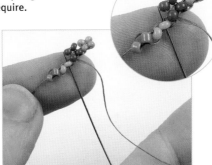

1 Pick up a new pair of beads to match the third and fourth beads in your base row. Take your needle and thread down the fourth bead in your base row and pull the thread tight.

2 Thread up through the fifth bead in your base row to be in the correct position to continue adding beads. Repeat steps 1 and 2 to finish beading your row. Ensure, every time you pick up a pair of beads, that they match the pair in the ladder base they will sit on top of.

232

Ending your herringbone row

There are three different methods for turning at the end of your row so that you are in the correct position to continue beading. Which one you choose is up to you. Each turn begins with you having added the last pair of beads in the previous row and exiting the edge bead in your ladder stitch base or previous row of herringbone.

THREAD OUTSIDE TURN

This is the easiest turn to complete but leaves a thread sitting on the outside of your work.

1 Thread around the outside edge of your work and through the last bead added in the previous row.

2 If you want to hide the thread along the edge, pick up some beads to cover it before threading through.

WEAVING THROUGH TURN

This is slightly trickier to bead and can lead to the end beads lying straight and not slanted.

AROUND A LOOP

This is reasonably easy to bead but not as secure as threading through a bead.

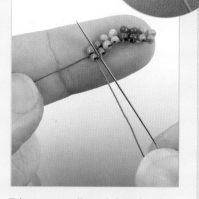

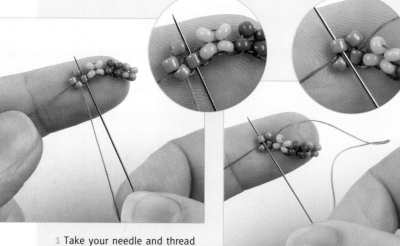

1 Take your needle and thread up through the next bead in on your ladder stitch base or previous row of herringbone.

2 Thread through the last bead added in the last row of herringbone.

Take your needle and thread under the loop connecting the nearest beads in your ladder base or previous row of herringbone and back through the last bead added.

233

Working a new row of herringbone stitch

After you have beaded your turn, you can continue beading to make your work as long as you require. Beading subsequent rows uses exactly the same steps you have already performed so it is easy for you to carry on.

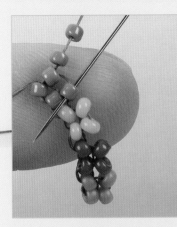

3 Repeat steps 1 and 2 to bead the remainder of your row and then turn using your turn of choice.

1 Pick up two beads to match the bead you are currently exiting. Thread down the second bead in on your previous row to secure the new beads.

2 Thread up through the third bead in your previous row to be in the correct position to continue beading.

234

Stacks, columns, rows, pairs, and rungs

The annotated bead pattern below will help you to use beading terminology such as "stacks," "columns," "rows," "pairs," and "rungs" more confidently when you attend beading circles or classes. Jargon like this can be difficult to learn at first, but you'll soon become familiar with these essential words.

Rungs are the individual beads in your ladder stitch base.

Pairs are the groups of two beads you add at each step.

Stacks are the lines of pairs of beads.

Rows are the line of beads going from one side to another.

Columns are the lines of single beads that form one half of a pair.

235

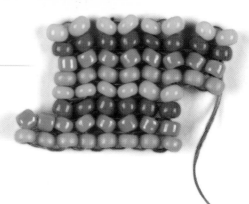

Increasing and decreasing herringbone

Herringbone can be increased and decreased along each edge, and you can also increase within your work.

INCREASING AND DECREASING AT THE EDGE

Adding or losing stacks of beads at the edge of your work is the easiest way to increase or decrease when beading with herringbone stitch.

1 To decrease at an edge simply stop beading a row before you reach the end of it, turn, and continue with the next row.

2 To increase at an edge, after you have added your last pair of beads in a row, ladder stitch a new pair of beads to the edge of the previous row and then herringbone stitch a new pair on top of these to finish the row.

INCREASING BETWEEN THE STACKS

This method leaves the edges of your work the same but adds a new set of stacks over a couple of rows of beadwork. How many rows of single and double beads you add before you bead into them is up to you, and depends how rapidly you want the increase to occur.

Working from right to left, thread up this bead from the bottom, and pick up a new pair of beads.

Thread up through this bead to continue your row.

Thread down into this bead to secure your new pair.

1 When you add a pair of beads, thread down through your bead to attach as with regular herringbone. Pick up a new bead and then thread up through the next bead to position yourself to continue. Repeat, picking up a new bead as many times across your row as you require.

2 For the next row, bead herringbone stitch as usual. When you reach your previous single bead increase, pick up one or two beads to lie on top of the extra one in the previous row. Continue adding rows of one or two beads, but only two if you have already added two.

3 Once you are happy with the increase and that your work is lying flat, as you bead the next row, treat the pair of new beads as a new herringbone stack and bead into them. Once beaded into, these beads will begin to lie in the distinctive herringbone pattern.

DECREASING BETWEEN STACKS

This method of decreasing leaves the edges of your work the same but removes pairs of beads from within the piece.

Skip over your missing beads and pull tight.

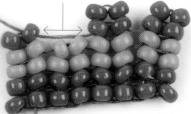

Miss adding a stack here? Instead, simply thread through without any beads.

1 Bead your row using regular herringbone stitch but when you meet the point you want to decrease, thread through your work as though you were working a herringbone stitch, but with no beads on your thread. Finish your row as usual and turn.

2 Begin the next row as usual and when you meet the point with the missing beads, simply skip over them and weave up through the next bead in the next stack to continue.

Peyote stitch

Peyote stitch is one of the most commonly used bead stitches around the world. The name "peyote" derives from America, when it was used to decorate objects used in Native American peyote ceremonies. Based on a simple rhythm of creating spaces and then filling those spaces, once it is started it is relatively easy to bead. However, some people find the start difficult, so pay attention.

SEE ALSO:

Quick tips and
tricks, page 91
Brick stitch,
page 96

236

Designing with peyote stitch

The beads in a row of peyote stitch sit beside each other, but each one is offset from the ones to its side, which gives the work its distinctive appearance. Pieces of peyote stitch are reasonably secure, as each bead is joined to the ones either side in separate rows.

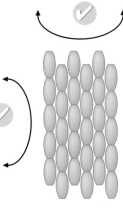

A piece of flat peyote stitch will bend along its width, and along its length.

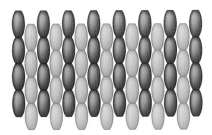

With peyote stitch you can bead stripes along the length. Simply pick up alternate beads in different colors. Add subsequent rows with the beads that sit behind them.

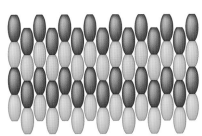

Stripes across the width will be zigzagged. Also note that the top and bottom edge won't be straight but the sides will be. If you want stripes that go straight across, bead using brick stitch.

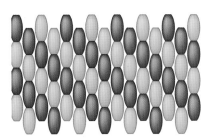

Diagonal stripes will work because the beads in the different rows are offset.

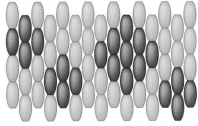

You can also bead triangles and diamonds into your work. Experiment to see which you like the look of best.

Need horizontal stripes?
Note that a piece of peyote stitch turned on its side resembles a piece made using brick stitch, so if you want horizontal stripes, consider using brick stitch instead.

237

Even-count or odd-count?

Flat peyote stitch comes in two different variants: even- or odd-count. Which one you bead depends on how many beads you want across the width of your beadwork. Even-count is easier to bead, while odd-count has a trickier turn at the end of every other row. Both can be used for symmetrical pieces of work, the only difference being that odd-count will give you a central bead or "column."

EVEN-COUNT
This is the easiest method of flat peyote stitch to bead, and is the best one to begin with.

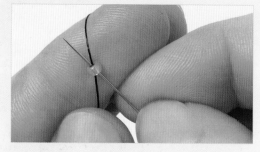

1 Thread your needle with a workable length of thread and add a stop bead. Pick up an even number of beads to create the width you would like and slide them down to your stop bead. These are the beads in your first two rows.

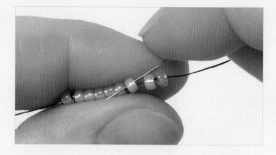

2 Pick up one more bead—using a different color may help you to see what you are beading more clearly. Take your needle and thread back through the second to last bead you picked up in step 1, the last bead of row 2. The new bead you have added is the first of row 3.

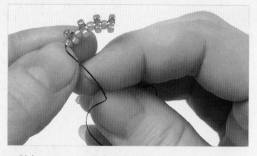

3 Pick up one more bead, in the second color if using, and missing the next bead you picked up in step 1, go through the next. This means you miss the bead in row 1 and go through the one in row 2. Repeat this pattern of picking up one, missing one, and going through one all the way along your row. You have now created the gaps you will fill with beads in each subsequent row.

5 Continue adding new beads along this row, only going through the beads that stick up, which will be the beads in your third row. If you used two different-colored beads you'll notice you only go through beads of the second color. Continue this pattern of adding rows by filling the gaps until your work is the length you require.

4 Pick up one bead in the first color—this is the first bead of your fourth row. Take your needle and thread back through the last bead added in the previous row.

ODD-COUNT

Trickier to bead than even-count, this method has a figure-eight turn at the end of every other row to get you into the correct position to bead your next row. To make this method easier to understand, make sure you're comfortable with even-count peyote stitch first.

1 Thread your needle with a workable length of thread and add a stop bead. Pick up an odd number of beads to create the width you would like, and slide them down to your stop bead. These beads form your first two rows. Using regular peyote stitch, bead along your row until you are two beads from the end and can't easily add another bead. Without picking up a new bead, thread down through the next two beads—the end beads of rows 2 and 1. Pick up one new bead—this will be the last bead of your third row—and thread back through the second bead in from the edge of your work (the last bead in row 2) and the lowest bead in the next pair (the second to last bead of the first row). You have now finished beading your third row.

2 You now need to reposition your needle and thread so you are in the correct place to continue beading. Pass your needle and thread through the bead above the one you are currently exiting. Ensure you are now working toward the end of your row.

3 Thread through the next beads along—the last beads in rows 1 and 2.

4 Thread back through the last new bead added, ensuring you are now pointing toward the body of your piece. You are now in the correct position to add a new bead and bead your fourth row.

Odd-count peyote stitch is ideal for designing pieces with a central bead in them.

238   Counting rows

It's very easy to lose count of how many rows you have beaded using peyote stitch, as the rows are offset. This means that, unlike in, say, brick stitch, counting the edge beads along one side doesn't give you the number of rows you have beaded. Instead you need to count both sides. There are three different counting methods:

COUNT BOTH SIDES
Simply count the beads along both edges and add the totals to get your total number of rows.

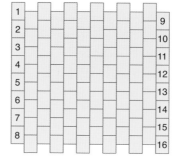

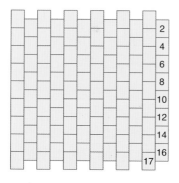

COUNT ONE SIDE
Count the beads along the edge where the top bead sits lower than the other edge. Count in pairs and then if at the end there's a row lower than this add it on for your total row figure.

COUNT ON THE DIAGONAL
Begin to count at the top edge bead and then count diagonally down your work until you reach the last row.

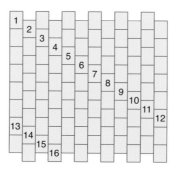

239   First rows

In peyote stitch, the beads you pick up first will determine the width of your work and form the first and second rows of your piece.

240   Stop bead start

Adding a stop bead at the start of your peyote stitch will help you to get the tension you want, as the first rows move about a lot. You may find that after adding the third row, sliding your stop bead back toward your beadwork helps as well. You can also use the stop bead as the first bead in your first row.

Increasing and decreasing peyote

Peyote stitch is ideal for increasing and decreasing within your work. Simply follow the steps below and in no time your work will be growing just as you want it to.

INCREASING

When increasing within your work, you want to ensure you keep the increase gradual so that your work remains flat. The best way to do this is to spread your increases out over many rows so they don't happen too rapidly.

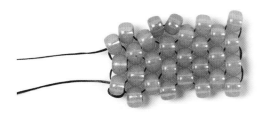

1 Bead peyote stitch until you reach the point at which you want the increase to occur. At this point, use two beads for the next stitch instead of the usual one.

2 On your next row, split the two beads with one bead and, for the row after, bead peyote stitch as normal. Now, your increase is finished.

DECREASING

Just as with increasing, when you're decreasing in peyote stitch, try to stagger your decreases out over lots of rows so that your work doesn't buckle or bulge. Some unevenness is to be expected as your work needs to adjust to having fewer beads in some rows—work slowly and neatly to minimize this.

1 Bead peyote stitch until you reach the point at which you want the decrease to occur. At this point, simply thread through your beads, but without picking up a new bead.

2 Pull your thread firmly to reduce the gap as much as possible. Note that, as you bead the next few rows, this will also bring the space closer. When beading the next row, place one bead over the decrease and, on the row after, bead peyote stitch as usual to complete the decrease.

These bracelets mix 1- and 2-drop beading by combining large cylinder beads with smaller ones.

SEE ALSO:

Working with thread,
page 88
Quick tips and tricks,
page 91
Tension tips, page 113
Tubular beadwork,
page 119
Loom work, page 136

Square stitch

Square stitch is ideal for making patterns and designs—the beads sit squarely next to each other so planning is easier than other stitches. It is a repetitive, easy-to-learn stitch. It is obvious where to add a new bead, so is ideal for a beginner. This stitch is named for the fact that the beads sit squarely next to and above each other.

242
Designing with square stitch

The beads in a piece of finished square stitch, just as in a piece of finished loom work, sit square to each other in a straight row. Pieces of square stitch are especially durable as the threads pass through each bead a few times.

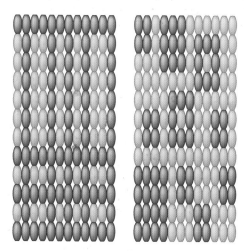

You can bead blocks, squares, and rectangles with square stitch. Add different colors in different rows or blocks following the patterns above, or create your own designs.

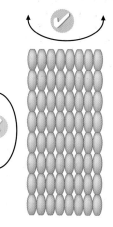

Square stitch and loom work will both bend easily across the length but not along the width.

243
Square stitch vs loom work

Square stitch and loom work both give you a finished piece of work that looks the same. Square stitch and loom work both lend themselves to using cross stitch or tapestry patterns as inspiration. However, be aware that as seed beads are not square but are more rectangular in shape, your finished piece will be taller than if made with loom work. Which one you choose to use is based on personal preference and the project involved. To help you choose, the pros and cons of each method are below.

Technique	Pros	Cons
Square stitch	• No set-up required. • Unlike loom work, there isn't the problem of having lots of thread ends to deal with. • No size limitations.	• Slower than loom work.
Loom work	• Quicker to bead than square stitch.	• A loom is required. • Size limits are based on the size of your loom. • Set-up and planning required.

244

Beading square stitch

Square stitch is a repetitive stitch to bead. The same steps are repeated throughout until your work is the length you require. You can choose to turn your work after each row, or to always work away from or toward yourself. Beading square stitch is ideal for beading large panels or pictures as it is easy to bead and maintains a regular size.

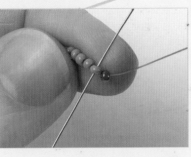

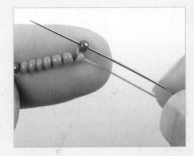

1 Thread your needle with a comfortable working length of thread and add a stop bead. Pick up the number of beads you require for the width of your piece and slide these down to your stop bead. These beads form your first row.

2 Pick up one new bead; this is the first bead of your second row. Circle through the last bead of your first row to attach the new bead.

3 Circle through the new bead to bring yourself back into position to continue beading.

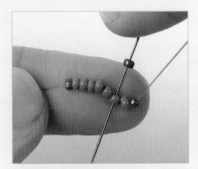

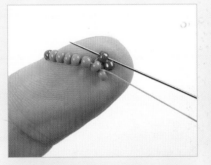

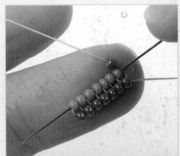

4 Pick up a new bead; this is the second bead of your second row. Circle back through the second last bead of the first row to join the two beads.

5 Circle through the new bead to be in the correct place to continue beading.

6 Continue to pick up new beads, attach them to the appropriate bead in the previous row, and then circle back through the new bead to be in the correct position to continue. You can now weave through the previous row to bring all the beads in line. Simply circle through all the beads in the previous row, and then all the beads in the new row will be back in position to continue beading. Simply repeat steps 2–6 to add new beads and rows until your work is the length you require.

245

To secure or not to secure?

Weaving through your previous rows is common in square stitch. This is because the first few rows can be quite loose, and as you continue beading and the rows tighten, you can find they look uneven. Other reasons for doing this are to add security to your work and to create a tighter tension. To weave through, simply finish beading a row, then circle all the way along the previous row, and the row just added, to be back in the correct position to continue, as in step 6. Whether you do this is entirely up to you and depends on the look and tension you are after.

246

Increasing and decreasing square stitch

Square stitch can be used to make a flat square piece of beadwork but, with some increasing and decreasing, you can shape your work to make it more interesting.

INCREASING ON THE OUTSIDE EDGE
This increases the length of a row while keeping your work flat.
The basic technique adds one extra bead to the length of your row.

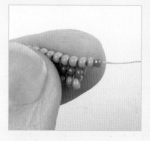

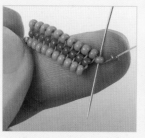

Increasing by more than one bead

To increase by more than one bead, simply pick up your two beads and circle through the first one. Then pick up two more beads and again circle through the first one. Continue adding pairs of beads until you have increased by as many as you require then circle through the second bead of the last pair you picked up. Finally, thread through all of the second beads to be back in position to continue with the row.

1 At the end of a row, on the side where you want to add an increase, pick up two new beads. One of these will be the last bead of the row you are currently on and one will be the first bead of the next row.

2 Circle back through the first bead to secure the beads together.

3 Circle through the second bead to be in the correct position to continue beading and work on the next row.

DECREASING ON THE OUTSIDE EDGE
You can decrease on an edge by as many beads as you choose to.

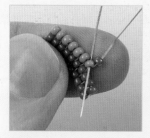

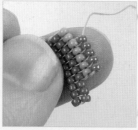

1 Bead your row as normal and then weave back through the previous row. When you weave back through the last row added, stop after you have gone through the last bead you want to attach your new one to. For example, if you want to decrease your row by three beads, stop when you have exited the fourth bead from the end.

2 Pick up a new bead and attach it to the appropriate bead in the previous row as in regular square stitch. Circle through the new bead to be in the correct position to continue.

3 Continue adding beads as in regular square stitch until you have added as many as you require. You can decrease at the second end by simply not stitching a new bead onto the last bead or beads as required.

4 Continue beading your next row using regular square stitch, or decrease as needed.

Tension tips

SEE ALSO:

Working with thread,
page 88
Quick tips and tricks,
page 91

Keeping the right tension in your beadwork is very important. If you want your necklace to curve elegantly around your neck, the tension needs to be looser than that of a three-dimensional vessel that needs to stand up, so you need to consider this before you begin a new piece. Everyone's natural beading tension will be different, and you will find it will also change from project to project. There are lots of tips to help you get the exact result you're looking for.

247 Tightening your work

If your work is looser than you'd like, the following tips will help to tighten it.

EXTRA THREADS
Using more than one thread fills the holes of your beads and will stiffen your work. Beware, though, that this is not always possible if using beads with small holes (e.g. size 15) or stitches where you thread through the same beads lots of times (i.e. square stitch or right-angle weave).

WEAVING BACK THROUGH
Weaving back through your work to retrace your steps fills the holes in the same way as using more than one thread does thereby stiffening your work.

HOLDING YOUR WORK
Holding your work as you bead will not only mean you work a lot quicker, as you don't waste time stopping to find your place again; it will also increase and regulate the tension throughout the piece.

SMALLER BEADS
If you use smaller beads with the same-sized thread, you'll find that your tension will tighten without you having to do any extra work, as the thread fills the holes more and means the beads can move around less.

BEADING WAX
Beading wax coats your thread and makes it slightly sticky. This means that the threads stick to each other inside the beads and have a similar effect to using more than one thread at a time.

STOP BEAD
Adding a stop bead at the start of your work will help you to tighten your tension as you can tighten your work against it when you start.

MATTE BEADS
Beads with shiny surfaces slide against each other whereas those with matte finishes, especially etched beads, "grip" each other and will make your work less floppy.

ADDING SUBSEQUENT ROWS
As you bead your piece you'll find that adding subsequent rows will tighten those previously added, so never judge your tension until you have beaded more than a few rows.

248 Loosening your work

If your work is tighter than you'd like, the following tips will help to loosen it.

BIGGER BEADS
Using larger beads but the same thread, such as size 6 or 8 seed beads, will make your work floppier.

PUT YOUR WORK DOWN
Putting your work down frequently as you bead will mean the tension doesn't stay as tight.

SHINY BEADS
The surface on shiny beads means they slide against each other so they won't sit so tightly in your work and the finished pieces will be more flexible.

THREAD CONDITIONER
This works in the opposite way to beading wax. Conditioner coats your threads and makes them slide against each other, and as a result your work will be looser.

SEE ALSO:

Quick tips and tricks,
page 91
Tubular beadwork,
page 119

Right-angle weave

So-called because the beads you add lie at right angles to each other, this is widely thought of as being the hardest beadwork stitch to learn and because of this many people avoid it. However, a few simple tricks will soon help you to learn it and add it to your stitching repertoire.

249

Designing with right-angle weave

Right-angle weave is much harder to design with as the beads sit facing two different ways. However, this doesn't mean you can't add design to your work, just that you may need to think ahead a bit more. Pieces of right-angle weave are very durable as most beads are threaded through numerous times.

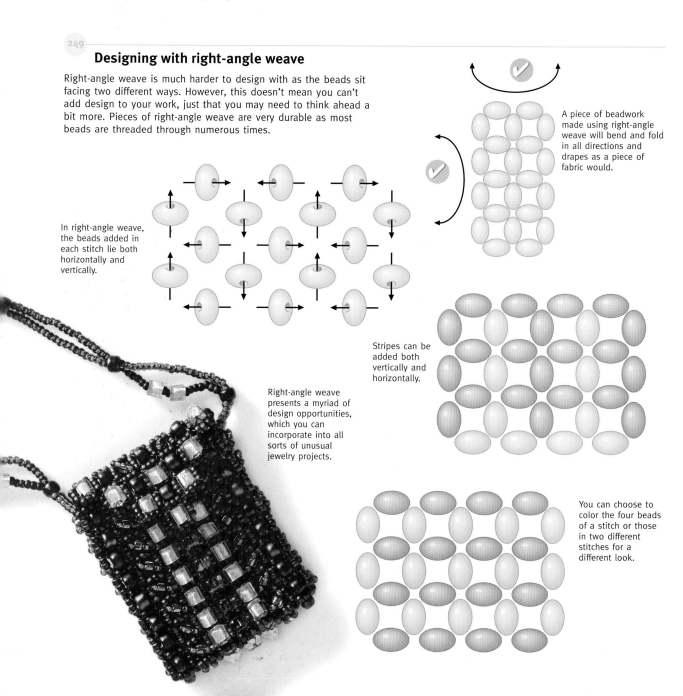

A piece of beadwork made using right-angle weave will bend and fold in all directions and drapes as a piece of fabric would.

In right-angle weave, the beads added in each stitch lie both horizontally and vertically.

Stripes can be added both vertically and horizontally.

Right-angle weave presents a myriad of design opportunities, which you can incorporate into all sorts of unusual jewelry projects.

You can choose to color the four beads of a stitch or those in two different stitches for a different look.

250

Beading right-angle weave

This is a tricky stitch at first as you don't pick up the same amount of beads for each step, or take the same thread path each time. It is easiest to learn this stitch if you remember that each stitch you make consists of two parts: adding the new beads and then getting into position to continue beading. Imagine that with each stitch and row you add you are building boxes with sides, tops, and bottoms.

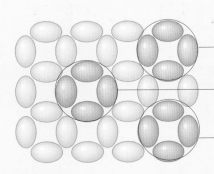

This box shares its bottom with the top of the one below.

This box shares all of its sides with other boxes.

This box shares its sides and top with other boxes but has its own bottom.

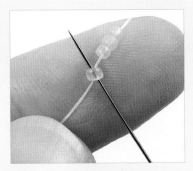

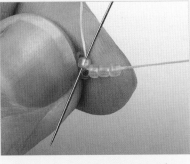

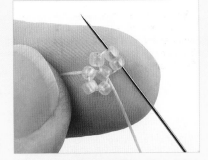

1 Thread your needle with a workable length of thread and pick up four seed beads (the first of these can be a stop bead which may help with your tension). Circle through the first bead again to join all the beads into a circle. This is your first box.

2 Pick up three beads. Your second box will share a side with the first so one less bead is needed. Circle through the bead you were exiting to join the second box to the first. Note that you will thread down this bead.

3 You now need to reposition yourself so you are in the correct place to continue. Thread through the next two beads: the bottom and second side of your new box. Always make sure you carry on threading in the same direction as you move to add the new box.

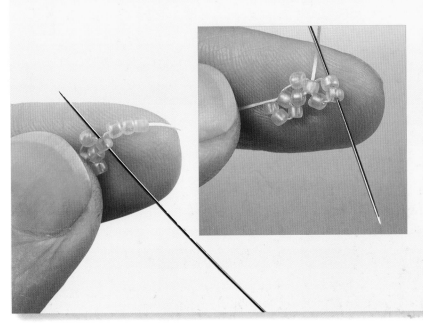

4 You will now add your third box and again, as it shares a side with the previous one, you only need to pick up three beads. Thread through the side bead you were exiting to join the new box. Note that this time you will thread up this bead. Whether you thread up or down alternates through your work. Circle through the next two beads—this will get you in the correct position to continue. Continue adding boxes and repositioning until your work is the width you require.

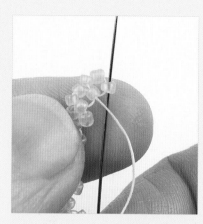

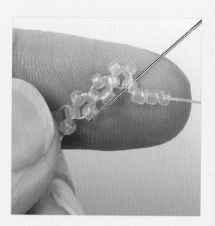

5 To add a new row, you need to get into the correct position. The bead type and bead count will depend on whether you have added an even or odd number of boxes to your first row. If you added an even number (shown above), you need to circle through three beads to be exiting the bottom bead of your last box.

If you added an odd number (shown above), you need to circle through one more bead to be exiting the bottom bead of your last box.

6 Your first box of this row will share the bottom of the last box you beaded as its top, so you only need to pick up three beads. Pick these up and then circle through the bead you were exiting—the bottom of the last box of the previous row. You have now added the first box of the second row.

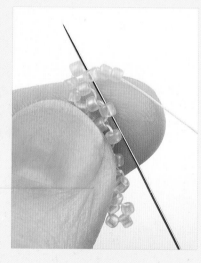

7 You now need to reposition to continue with this row. Depending on whether you added an even or odd number of boxes to the first row you will either: circle through to be exiting the bead that is the bottom bead of the box above where you will want to add your next box (if even), or: circle through to be exiting the side bead of the new box (if odd). Your next box will share a top with the box above and a side with the previous box, so you only need to pick up two beads to complete it. Thread on two beads. Thread through the appropriate beads to join to the side and bottom of the previous boxes. You have now added the second box of the second row. Reposition so you are exiting either the side bead of the new box or the bottom bead of the next box in the previous row—whichever you didn't exit through last time.

8 Continue adding boxes by picking up two beads and ensure you reposition each time by circling through either one or three beads alternately when exiting the side bead of the last box added. Note that for each subsequent row, the pattern is now the same. The first box always needs three new sides and each subsequent box only needs two.

251

2-drop and more

Using two or more beads in place of one, or even just one bugle bead, will give your work a more open look and, once mastered, you may find it easier to bead.

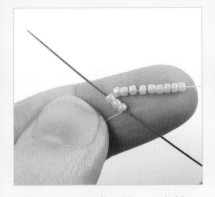

1 Thread your needle with a workable length of thread and pick up twelve beads, which will give you three beads for each box side. Circle through the first three beads to make a circle.

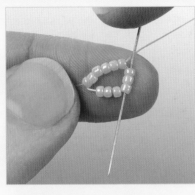

2 Circle through the next six beads (the three for the top and three for the next side) to be in the correct position to continue.

3 Pick up nine beads, for the bottom, side, and top of the next box, and circle through the three beads of the side you were exiting.

4 To reposition yourself, thread through the next two sets of three beads so you are exiting toward the top of the side of the second box.

5 Continue adding boxes with three beads on each side until your work is the width you require. Ensure that, at the end of the row, you reposition yourself to be exiting the bottom of the last box. Pick up nine beads to form the sides and bottom of the first box of the second row. Circle through the bottom beads of the last box on the first row.

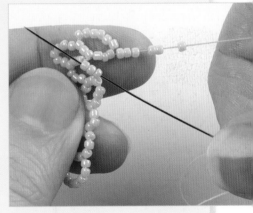

6 Reposition yourself as in regular right-angle weave so you are in the correct position to continue. Continue adding beads and repositioning, remembering that you now only need to pick up six beads each time to complete each box in the row.

252

Increasing and decreasing right-angle weave

Right-angle weave can be increased both within your work and on the edges. The combination of increases and decreases match with the stitch's natural fluidity, making it ideal for covering objects.

INCREASING ON THE EDGE

Adding extra sections to the side of your work will increase the width whilst leaving the main body of your piece unaffected.

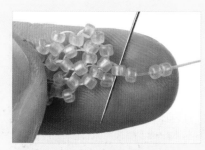

Add an extra box onto either edge of your work by picking up three beads and circling through the bead you exited. You can reposition yourself and add more groups of three beads to add as many extra boxes as you require.

DECREASING ON THE EDGE

Beading less sections at the sides of your work will cause it to shrink widthways without any impact on the rest of your work.

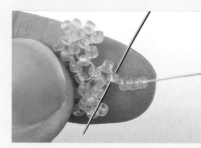

To decrease, simply don't add boxes all the way along a row but instead begin your next row down.

INCREASING WITHIN YOUR WORK

Bead as usual until you reach the point where you want to add an increase. Pick up one extra bead for the next box so that the bottom has two beads instead of one. Continue as usual. On the next row, when you reach the increase, add a new box onto each of the bottom beads of the box above to complete your increase.

DECREASING WITHIN YOUR WORK

Beading fewer sections across the width of your work will decrease its width but can also cause your work to ruffle. Keep your increases gradual by spacing them out across different rows.

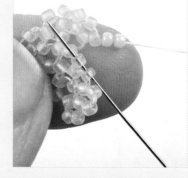 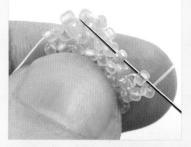

1 Work regular right-angle weave until you reach the point where you want to decrease. Add your new box but attach it to the bottom bead of the box above and the next one along. Reposition and continue your row as normal.

2 Begin your next row and when you reach the decrease, simply bead onto the existing box to complete the decrease.

Tubular beadwork

Tubular beadwork uses all of your favorite beading stitches to create tube-shaped pieces of beadwork. Some beadwork is worked in exactly the same way when tubular as when flat, but there are exceptions. Read the instructions for each stitch to check for any differences and to make sure you're not caught out by any changes.

SEE ALSO:

Quick tips and tricks, page 91
Ladder stitch, page 94
Brick stitch, page 96
Peyote stitch, page 105
Herringbone stitch, page 100
Square stitch, page 110
Right-angle weave, page 114

253 Joining start rows

Some stitches, such as ladder stitch, square stitch, and right-angle weave, begin with a flat piece of work which is then joined into a tube. Make sure you pay attention as to whether you need to add new beads to complete the join or not and also make sure you don't twist the beadwork when joining the ends.

Step-up

Some stitches, such as peyote and herringbone, require a step-up at the end of each round to bring you into the correct position to continue your work. Always pay attention when reaching the end of your row so you don't miss this step-up by accident.

Ladder start

Brick and herringbone stitch both begin with a ladder stitch start. Just as with regular ladder stitch, this can be beaded using 1-drop (or more).

Joining your beads into a circle by weaving through them allows for more movement.

254 To knot or not?

When joining the beads together to begin your first row, you can either knot your thread or weave through all the beads again to join them into a circle. Knotting is secure but doesn't give you any scope for flexibility and movement in your work, and if you tie the knot in the wrong place your circle of beads won't be joined as you want them. Weaving through all the beads joins them into a circle but is less secure until you add more rows. However, it does give you some flexibility and means the beads can sit as they want to with some movement.

Joining your beads into a circle with a knot is secure.

255 Beading over a form

Some people find that beading over a form helps them to keep their work even and also to see exactly what they are doing and where to go next. Some people prefer to bead tubular work over their fingers. You can use any form that's the right size for the work you want to create.

Try beading over a narrow pencil or a large marker pen, a cardboard tube, a drinking straw, a chopstick, or even your fingers (below).

256

Tubular ladder stitch

As well as being a stitch in its own right, tubular ladder stitch is the start of tubular brick and herringbone stitches.

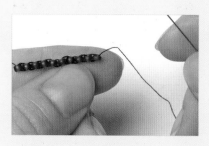

1 Work a piece of ladder stitch as long as is required.

2 Bring the two ends of your work together, ensuring it hasn't twisted at all, and circle through the first bead and then the last bead to join them together.

257

Tubular herringbone stitch

This builds from a tubular ladder stitch base, just as regular herringbone stitch builds from a regular ladder stitch base. However there is a step-up at the end of the row which you need to perform to ensure you are in the correct position to continue with your next row.

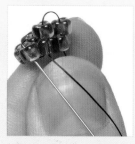 

1 Bead your ladder stitch base and join the ends together. Pick up two beads and thread down through the next bead along in your ladder base and then up through the next ladder base bead along, just as in regular herringbone stitch.

2 Continue adding pairs of beads using regular herringbone stitch all the way around to bead your row. Your step-up occurs as you finish adding your last pair of beads. Add the pair and thread down through the next ladder base bead as usual. However, you now need to thread up through the next ladder base bead, and the herringbone bead sitting directly on top of it. This is the first bead you picked up in this row. You are now in the correct position to begin your next row.

258

Tubular brick stitch

This builds from a tubular ladder stitch base, just as regular brick stitch builds from a regular ladder stitch base.

1 Bead your ladder stitch base and join the ends together. Pick up two beads and thread under the nearest thread loop. Take your needle and thread back through the second bead just added as in regular brick stitch. Continue adding seed beads using regular brick stitch.

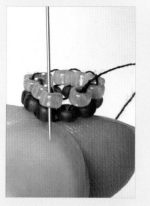

2 To end a row, add a bead to the last thread loop and then thread down the first bead, under the loop it is attached to and back through the first bead again. This joins the first and last bead of your row and stops any gaps developing. Continue beading rows of brick stitch, remembering to always pick up two beads at the start of a row.

259

Tubular peyote stitch

To begin, you thread on the beads for the first two rows at once, just as you do in regular peyote stitch.

1 Thread on an even number of beads and tie into a circle around a shaped form. Pick up one bead, and missing the next bead along, thread through the next. Repeat this pattern all the way around the circle.

2 To step-up at the end of the row, take your needle through the next bead to finish your stitch and row, and then thread through the first new bead you picked up in this, the third row. You are now in the correct position to add a new bead and continue beading.

260

Following a chart

When beading anything in tubular beadwork, especially when following a chart, you need to be aware that the first bead to be picked up moves along a space each time in both peyote and brick stitch. Some charts will highlight this bead for you, but if it's not obvious, you may find it easier to draw on your chart yourself.

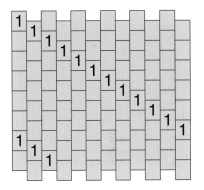

261

Tubular square stitch

This is beaded in exactly the same way as regular square stitch, then you simply join the row when you start.

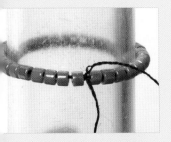

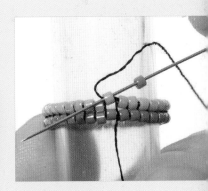

1 Begin by picking up all the beads you need for your first row. Join these into a circle by either tying a knot or weaving through the beads. Place this circle of beads around an appropriately-sized form.

2 Pick up a new bead—this is the first bead of your second row.

3 Circle through the bead you were exiting on the first row then circle through your new bead to be in position to continue beading.

4 Repeat steps 2 and 3 to complete the row. You can then weave through your previous row followed by the new one to secure the beads as in regular square stitch. Begin your next row by picking up a new bead and securing it to the bead you are exiting. Continue with square stitch to complete your work.

262

Tubular right-angle weave

This is slightly more complicated than the other tubular stitches, but if you can bead right-angle weave flat you can bead it tubular.

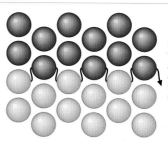

1 Bead a row of right-angle weave the width you require (using a shaped form if necessary) and join the end boxes by adding just the top and bottom beads. This last box will share the side beads with the two it unites.

2 Circle through your beads to be exiting a top or bottom bead in the direction you want to continue working. Pick up three new beads and circle through the bead you were exiting.

3 Reposition to continue and add new boxes, remembering that you will only need two new beads for each one. To finish your row, bead the last box by only adding one new bead as it will share its sides and bottom with previous boxes. Reposition to continue and carry on adding rows.

263

Making tubes

If you don't want to work in a tubular form, you can always bead a piece of flat beadwork and join it into a tube afterward. Some stitches, such as square, brick, and peyote can have this easily done by joining or "zipping" up the edges, whereas right-angle weave will need extra beads added for this to work.

Flat pieces of peyote stitch can have their top and bottom zipped into a tube as long as you have beaded an even number of rows.

Joining the edges of right-angle weave requires extra beads to form extra boxes.

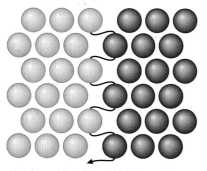

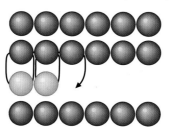

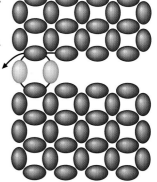

The sides of flat pieces of brick stitch can be zipped up by weaving from one edge of your work to the other to join it into a tube.

To join pieces of square stitch into a tube, simply weave through your work as though you were adding a new row with new beads, but instead thread through the beads at the edges.

SEE ALSO:

Seed beads and more, page 12

Spiral rope

Spiral rope is an endlessly versatile stitch that lends itself to lots of experimentation with the beads you use. Although it is ideal for beginners, some people do find the first few steps hard. Follow a few simple rules and you'll soon be spiraling away. Spiral rope is made up of two parts: the central core and the outer spiral. The type and number of beads you use for each step is entirely up to you. The only requirement is that the core beads can be threaded through at least three times.

Advantages of spiral

Spiral rope has many advantages:

Any way is the right way
If you do put spiral rope down and forget which was the top and which was the bottom, it doesn't matter. Each end will be the same, so you can carry on working from either end—as long as you follow the golden rules (see right).

Bead quantities
You can choose exactly how many beads you feature in your inner core and your outer spiral but remember that you will need at least three times as many beads for the outer spiral as you do for the core, so make sure you have enough when you begin.

The golden rules

There are three rules to follow to make your spiral work:

Always put each new spiral on top of the previous ones
To help you do this, it's easiest to always place each new spiral under the thumb on your non-dominant hand (i.e. your left hand if you're right-handed). Not doing this will cause your work to get very confused and tangled very quickly.

Thread through the same amount
Make sure that if you go through three core beads at the start, you thread through this amount at each step.

Always work in the same direction
If you're holding your work and threading up from the bottom, make sure you do this all the way along. Not doing this will create loops over your beadwork, not the smooth outer spiral you're looking for.

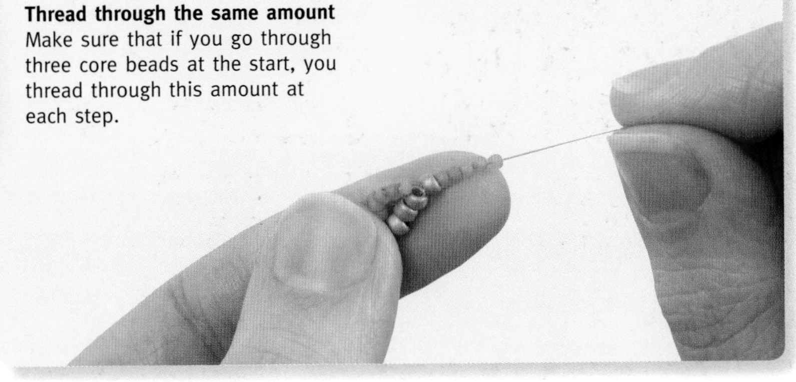

266

Beading spiral rope

Begin with a small number of beads and then you can move on to the endless experimentation that spiral rope allows. Size 8 and size 11 seed beads are ideal for making your first piece.

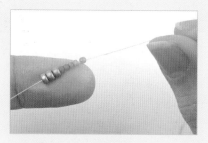

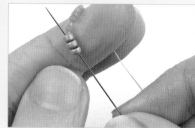

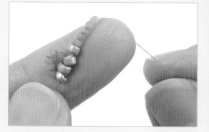

1 Begin with a comfortable working length of thread. Pick up three size 8 core beads and five size 11 outer spiral beads.

2 Circle through the core beads and then hold your work with the outer spiral sitting under the thumb of your non-dominant hand.

3 Pick up one core bead and five outer spiral beads and slide these down to your work.

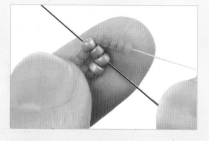

4 Thread up through the top two core beads, missing the bottom one, and then through the new core bead picked up. This means you are again threading through three core beads as you did in step 2.

5 Place the new outer spiral beads so they sit under your thumb on top of the previous ones.

6 Pick up one core bead and five outer spiral beads and slide them down to your work.

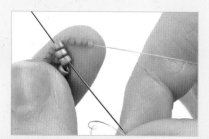

7 Thread up through the top two core beads in the piece already beaded, missing the bottom two, and then through the new core bead picked up. Place the new outer spiral beads on top of the previous ones.

8 Repeat steps 6 and 7 until your piece is as long as you require.

How many times?
How many times you thread through your core beads is easy to calculate. It's simply the number of beads in each step of your core.

Four size 8 beads for the core and three size 11 beads, a size 6, and three more size 11 beads make up the beaded chain of this necklace.

Spiral variations

Playing around with the size and type of beads can really alter the finished look.

Multicolored drops on every row add color as well as texture to these pieces.

Using three different colors in your outer spiral, with each color picked up in order, adds stripes that spiral around your work.

Instead of multiple beads in the outer spiral, why not use one long bead?

Adding a drop bead every third outer spiral adds texture to this necklace.

Adding a dagger bead every seventh outer spiral makes a necklace where they sit along the bottom edge.

Keeping your outer spiral plain but changing the color of your core beads adds a different look.

FIX IT

268   **Does your spiral look like this?**

If your spiral rope is confusing to look at, you have not placed each subsequent outer spiral on top of the previous ones. Undo the steps until your work looks correct and start again.

Four size 11 beads for the core and three size 11 beads for the outer spiral give a more delicate look.

269

Double spiral rope

If you like spiral rope, then you'll love double spirals. For double spiral, your core beads are threaded through double the amount of times as in regular spiral rope, so you will need to use a size 8 seed bead or larger to ensure the holes are big enough.

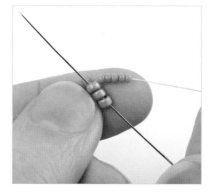

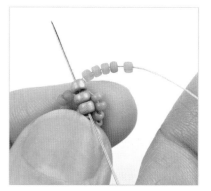

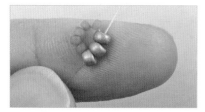

1 Pick up three size 8 beads for the core and five size 11 beads for your first outer spiral. Circle through the core beads.

2 Turn your work so that the outer spiral already added sits away from you. Pick up five size 11 seed beads in your second outer spiral color. Circle back through all of the core beads again. Using a different color for the two different outer spirals not only makes it easier for you to see what you're doing but creates a great look as they spiral around each other.

3 Turn your work so that your first outer spiral faces you and sits under the thumb of your non-dominant hand. Pick up one core bead and five of the beads you used for your first outer spiral. Slide the beads down and circle through the top two core beads already there and the new one just added. Place this new outer spiral on top of the first one.

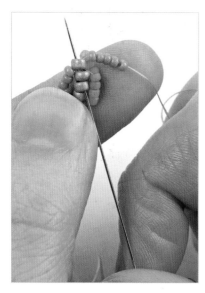

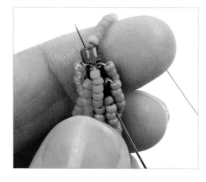

5 Repeat steps 3 and 4 until your work is the length you require, ensuring you turn it every time so that each outer spiral of a different color only sits on those of the same color.

4 Turn your work so the second outer spiral faces you and sits under your non-dominant thumb. Pick up just the beads needed for the next piece of your outer spiral and thread up through the top three core beads. Now you will only pick up a new core bead every time you add the first set of outer spirals. Essentially for every two outer spirals, you only add one core bead.

TRY IT

270　**Triple spiral rope**

If double has you hooked, why not be even more adventurous and go for a triple spiral rope?

Beading triple spiral
Bead a triple spiral just as you would bead a double, but make sure you turn your work around a third of the way between each different outer spiral. As you go through each core bead three

times more than with regular spiral rope, you need to ensure you use one with an extra-large hole, so use at least a size 6 seed bead or a double cylinder.

Quadruple spirals
Why stop at three? Try using the same technique to add four or more outer spirals to a piece.

Chains

As well as specific beading stitches, seed bead work is also made up of lots of different chains, all of which can be used to make beautiful jewelry. Each chain cries out to be experimented with, so play around with the shape, size, scale, and color of the beads. Don't feel limited to the specific instructions shown here—get your beads out and have fun.

SEE ALSO:

Quick tips and tricks, page 91
Tension tips, page 113
Moving on in beadweaving, page 145

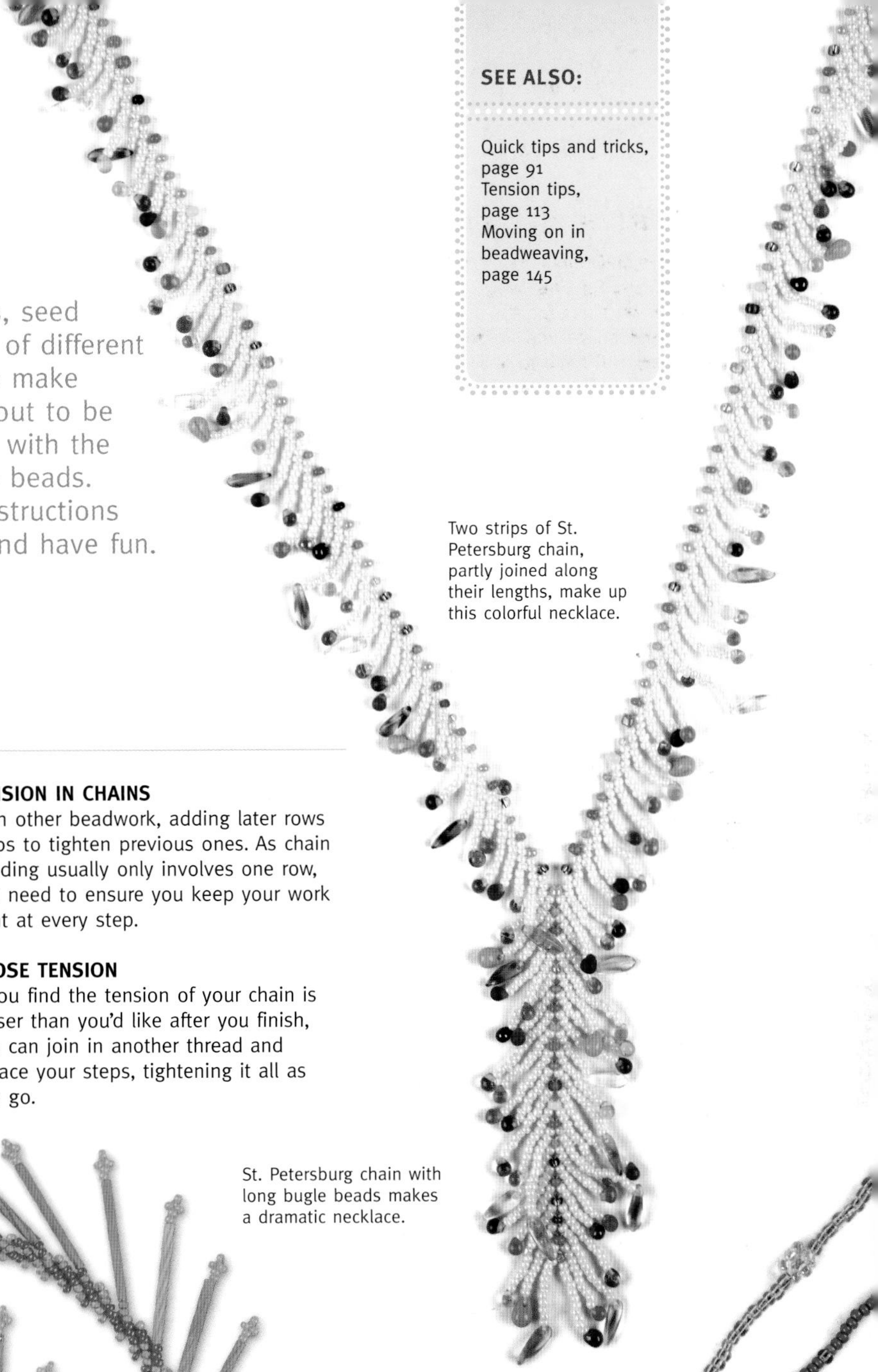

Two strips of St. Petersburg chain, partly joined along their lengths, make up this colorful necklace.

Basic beading chains

Chains are slightly different to beading stitches because they are not used to make different items—the chains are an end unto themselves. That is, you wouldn't usually use daisy, Nepal, or St. Petersburg chain to stitch a vessel.

TENSION IN CHAINS

With other beadwork, adding later rows helps to tighten previous ones. As chain beading usually only involves one row, you need to ensure you keep your work tight at every step.

LOOSE TENSION

If you find the tension of your chain is looser than you'd like after you finish, you can join in another thread and retrace your steps, tightening it all as you go.

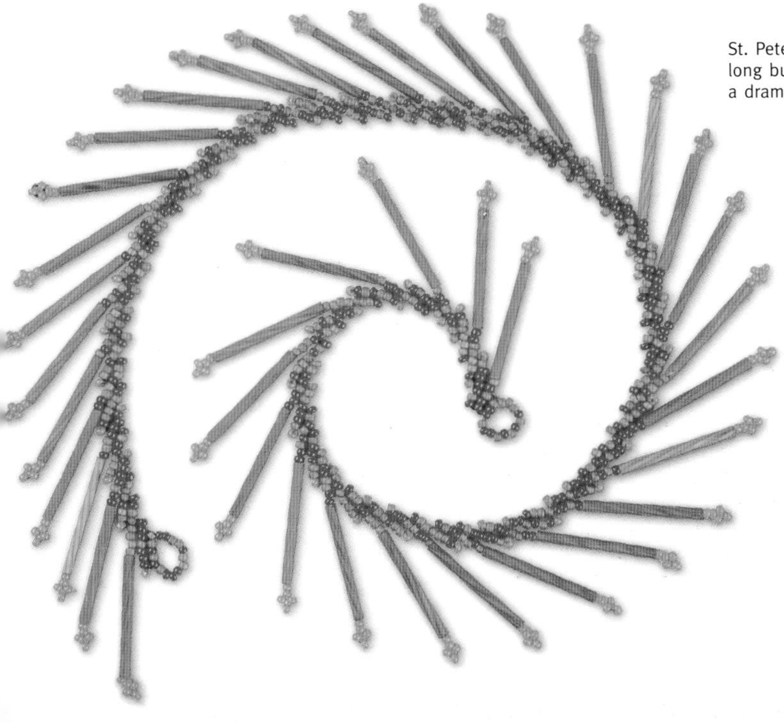

St. Petersburg chain with long bugle beads makes a dramatic necklace.

Daisy chains make a pretty, floral piece of beadwork.

272

Daisy chain

A pretty chain with many variations, daisy chain is an ideal chain to begin with. There are three different sections in the chain: the stems, the petals, and the daisy center, so you can use one, two, or three different colors. You can even use a different set of colors for each flower as you go along.

1 Thread your needle with a comfortable working length of thread and add a stop bead. Pick up eight stem beads and six petal beads. Circle through the first petal bead to join them into a circle.

2 Pick up one center bead and thread through the fourth petal bead in the same direction you previously threaded through it.

3 Pick up eight stem beads and six petal beads. Thread back through the first petal bead to join them into a circle.

4 Repeat steps 2 and 3 until your work is as long as you require.

Use beads in complementary colors such as green and red for a striking effect.

FIX IT

273   Not enough petals?

If you use a larger bead for the center, you will need extra petal beads to fit around it. Calculate how many you will need before you start.

274

Nepal chain

Another flower-patterned chain, this one is a bit more complicated than a daisy chain. This chain has two different parts: the stems and the flowers. You can also add in a third color to make some of the flowers into leaves. As in all beadwork, experimenting will give you lots of different looks.

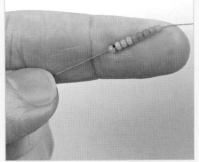

1 Thread your needle with a comfortable working length of thread and add a stop bead. Pick up three stem beads and five flower or leaf beads.

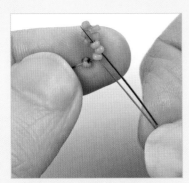

2 Thread back through all the stem beads and then back again through the second and third one.

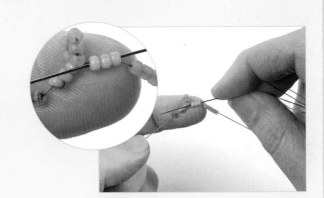

3 Pick up three stem beads and five petal or leaf beads. Pull the beads close against the previous set to keep the tension tight. Pass the needle back through the three stem beads. Pull tight.

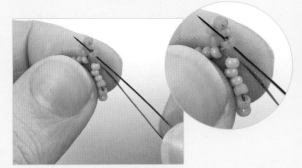

4 Thread through the first flower or leaf bead from the first set to join the second set to it.

5 Repeat steps 3 and 4 until your work is the length you want it to be.

275

St. Petersburg chain

This is a more complicated chain where you pick up the different beads in different places, which may not feel right at first. But persevere! It is an attractive chain which is worth the work. The chain uses beads in three different places: the main body, as a turn bead, and the "skip bead." These can all be the same color and shape or you can play around with changing them for a different look.

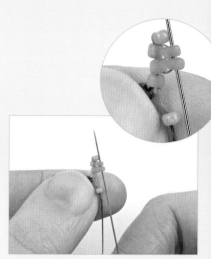

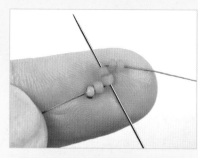

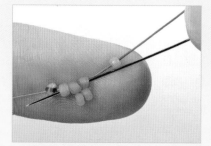

1 Thread your needle with a comfortable working length of thread and add a stop bead. Pick up five main beads, miss the first one added, and circle through the next two.

2 Pick up one turn bead and thread back through the three main beads you are currently exiting.

3 Pick up one skip bead and thread down the two main beads that sit next to the three you just threaded through.

STACKS

These steps refer to "stacks" to make it easier to understand where to go next. If you look at what has been beaded so far, the work comprises of two stacks. The first one is the row of three main beads and one turn bead, and the second one, which we are still beading, consists so far of a skipped bead and two main beads.

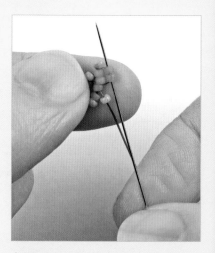

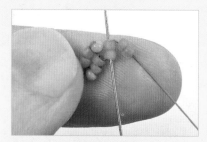

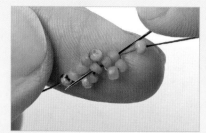

4 Pick up another four main beads and circle through the first two.

5 Pick up a turn bead and thread back up three main beads.

6 Pick up a skipped bead and thread down the two main beads in the next stack.

7 Repeat steps 4–6 until your work is as long as you would like it.

276

Joining strips of St. Petersburg

Bead a strip of St. Petersburg chain of the length you require. Begin a second piece but stop after step 2. Instead of picking up a new bead as your skipped bead, thread through the skipped bead on your first strip. Continue in this pattern until the second strip is as long as the first.

This chain can also be joined lengthwise to give you a completely different look.

Small sections of St. Petersburg chain with an increasing amount of beads used for each turn section can be used to make feather motifs when joined. You will need to bead an extra central "fringe" to fill the final gap.

TRY IT

277 Chain techniques

There are a number of techniques you can try to give your work a different look.

A drop bead can be used as your turn bead to add extra texture.

Picking up more than one bead as your turn bead—in this case a long bugle bead and five seed beads—gives you a different look. For the picot ending miss the last three beads and thread back up the rest.

Use different-colored and shaped beads for your turn and skipped beads to jazz up your work.

SEE ALSO:

Cords, threads, and
memory wire, page 18
Essential findings,
page 40
Opening and closing
loops, page 82
Peyote stitch,
page 105
Tubular beadwork,
page 119

Finishing your beadwork

So far we have looked at all the different stitches and techniques essential to beading with seed beads. Now it's time to look at how to ensure that your work is finished with security and has the professional look you're after.

278
The essentials

When you're finishing your work, there are a number of essential details you want to consider:

Security
You don't want to lose your piece of jewelry while wearing it, so always ensure that every fastening is safely and securely attached.

Neatness
Seed beadweaving can often take many hours. Don't ruin the look by rushing the finishing so it is a noticeably different standard than the rest of your work.

No wear on the thread
The thread you use when beadweaving is fairly fragile and constant rubbing against metal findings can wear it down.

279
Bought or made findings?

The decision to use readymade findings or make your own is up to you and will depend on the project as well as the time and energy you want to devote to the piece.

	Pros	Cons
Bought findings	• Easy to find. • Easy to add to piece. • Securely made.	• Can be hard to find one to suit your beadwork. • Metal findings can rub against thread, wearing it down. • Magnetic clasps can result in work being lost.
Made findings	• More likely to match your work. • Aren't as obvious to the observer and therefore don't clash.	• Take more time to make and add to your workload.

By hiding your fastening, you can combine the best of both worlds and use the security of a purchased clasp, but add a beaded cover to hide it. Make a piece of tubular beadwork that will fit over your jewelry. If made flat, "zip" up the edges and slide onto your work.

You can finish your piece in all sorts of extravagant ways, adding tassels, end beads, and charms as you see fit. This flamboyant necklaces makes use of a bar and toggle fastening (page 134), which is disguised by a cluster of beads and charms.

A long piece of beadwork, or lariat, can be tied around the neck with no fastening needed.

280

Types of fastenings

There are so many ways of fastening your jewelry: use bought fastenings such as toggles and lobster clasps, hide your fastenings with tubular beadwork, or use no fastening at all.

Metal clasps are ideal to finish your jewelry as they are secure and easy to find. Just be sure to add them securely to your work and in a way less likely to wear down your thread. You can simply exit your beadwork, and thread through the attaching loop of your clasp. It is best to circle through the clasp and your work as many times as you can to add more security.

Before threading through your clasp you can add a piece of gimp onto your thread that will protect your thread from wear and tear. However, as you will only be able to thread through the gimp once, if the thread does break there's no back-up.

When threading from your work to your clasp, you can put some beads onto your thread. If these beads fit through the attaching hole in your clasp they will protect it from rubbing against your thread.

Add a jump ring through one of the beads in your work and use this to attach a clasp. The advantage is that your clasp won't rub against your thread—but you have to use a bead big enough to fit a jump ring into.

Even if the beads don't fit through the clasp, they will still add a more finished look to your work.

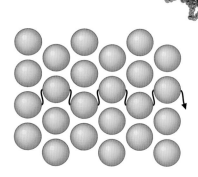

Beaded fastenings

Beaded fastenings can be used to add another decorative element to your work as their colors and textures will coordinate or contrast with the rest of your piece. However, they do take more time to make and you need to ensure you have made them securely.

ADDING A BEAD, BOBBLE, OR BUTTON

Choose a suitable button or bead and attach this to a short length of beads coming from your beadwork. At the other end make a loop large enough to fit over the bead or button, but small enough that it won't slip off too easily. Always attach your bead or button first and then make the loop. Never make the loop first as it's a lot harder to get the size correct this way.

MAKING YOUR OWN TOGGLE

1 Using even-count peyote stitch, bead a piece of work with an even number of rows.

2 "Zip" up the edges to make a bar.

Try embellishing the bar with beads as you attach it to your work.

MAKING YOUR OWN BOBBLE

1 If you don't have a suitable bead or button you can make your own bobble. Attach a bead with a large hole to your work. Pick up enough small beads to cover one side of the large bead and circle through the central bead.

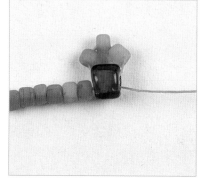

2 The right amount of beads will cover the side of the large bead without overflowing the ends too much.

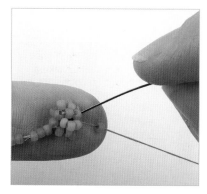

3 Repeat adding outer loops until your bobble is the size you require. Pick up one or more beads as a turn bead and then thread back into your work.

Following a chart

Following a bead chart can be very different from following written instructions. You need to pay special attention to each row and where the rows start as you work.

SEE ALSO:

Quick tips and tricks, page 91
Peyote stitch, page 105
Right-angle weave, page 114
Tubular beadwork, page 119

282 Peyote stitch charts

Always remember when looking at a peyote stitch chart that you pick up the first two rows at once when you begin in this stitch. So if you were following this chart, you would need to begin by picking up the beads with the darker outline in the order they are numbered.

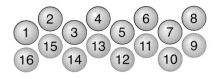

283 Moving the first bead

When following a chart for tubular beadwork, with some stitches you need to be aware that the first bead you pick up moves around your row. Some charts highlight this bead, as in the chart below, but if it's not obvious you may find it easier to mark on the chart yourself.

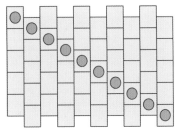

285 Reading charts

Charts for this stitch can be very confusing to look at but the example shows you in what order you would pick up the beads.

Bead charts often show beads as being round or square, when in reality seed and cylinder beads are longer—your work will turn out more rectangular than the chart suggests.

284 Coloring your chart

If it helps you to keep track of where you are as you work, color in each row or bead as you go. If you don't want to ruin your pattern, you can take a photocopy of it for this purpose or put it inside a plastic cover and write on the cover instead. (See page 25 for more information on magnetic boards.)

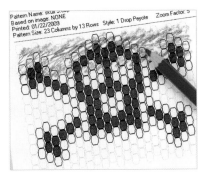

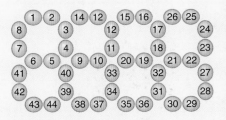

If beading this stitch with more than one bead on each side, your chart and progression of beads would look like this.

Loom work

Unlike other seed beadwork, which is all done by hand and held in the hand when working, loom work utilizes a tool—a loom—and is beaded on this loom until you come to finish your work. Loom work gives you the look of square stitch, but is a lot quicker to bead. However, after finishing your loom-work piece, you are left with lots of thread ends to weave in and finish off.

SEE ALSO:

Quick tips and tricks, page 91
Square stitch, page 110
Finishing your beadwork, page 132

286 Different loom-work methods

There are two main methods of beading on a loom. These are regular loom work and "pulled warp" loom work, also known as "pulled threads" or "endless warp." Regular loom work can be quicker to actually bead but at the end you will be left with all the warp threads to deal with. With pulled warps it can be slower to bead, because you have to be more careful as you work, but you deal with the problem of lots of warp threads by pulling them until you are left with just one long thread to deal with. But this method can be problematic and you need to work carefully to ensure you don't damage your work. Which method you choose depends on your personal preference, but to help you make your choice, check out the pros and cons below.

Technique	Pros	Cons
Regular loom work	• Less likely to make errors when finishing. • You don't have to be so careful when beading your work. • Can use either one long warp thread or individual ones.	• Lots of thread ends to weave in. • Slow to finish.
Pulled warp loom work	• Fewer thread ends to finish at the end.	• You need to be a lot more careful when beading that you don't pierce your thread. • You have to set your loom up with one long warp thread.

287 Setting up and getting started

The first step in loom work is setting up your loom. Exactly how you set it up depends on the method you've chosen.

Pulled warps: With pulled warps you need to ensure you have one long warp thread.
Regular loom work: With regular loom work you can have one long thread or lots of individual ones. The main thing you need to know is the exact bead width of your finished piece as this determines how many warps you need.

Working position: You will find it more comfortable and easier if you start your work at the end of the loom furthest away from you and work toward yourself. You will also find it easiest if you lay your beads down starting at the opposite side from your dominant hand—i.e. start at the left if you are right-handed.

Loom work is ideal for patterns and pictures as the beads sit square to each other in regular rows.

288

Individual warps

Decide how many beads will be in the width of your piece and cut this number of threads plus one more, and two extra for the edges. Ensure that these threads are all the length of your loom plus at least another 6in (15cm).

Extra threads

You always need to cut one extra warp thread than the width in beads for your piece but you can decide whether or not to use two threads for the end warps. Using two threads adds an extra layer of security to the edges of your piece but means two extra threads to deal with at the end.

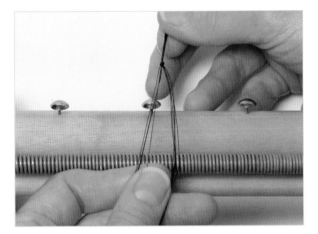

1 Knot all your threads together at one end using an overhand knot. Place this knot over one of the pegs at one end of your loom. If you are weaving a wider piece of loom work, you may want to separate your threads into different bundles and attach them to different pegs along the width of your loom.

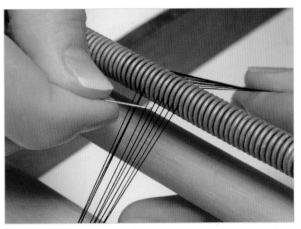

2 Using a needle or awl, separate the threads and position them in separate grooves along the width of your loom. Remember that if you used double threads for the edges you'll need to place two threads in each of the end grooves.

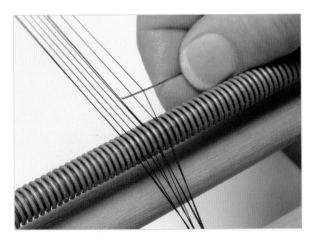

3 Tie the other ends of your threads together using an overhand knot around the peg at the other end of your loom. If your threads are a lot longer than your loom you will need to wind the roller at the loom end nearest you to tighten the threads. Do this until you remove any slack but don't tighten completely just yet. Make sure you wind the roller toward you and away from the main body of the loom.

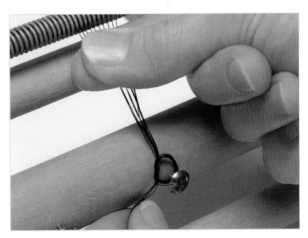

4 Use your needle or awl to place the threads into the appropriate grooves opposite the ones they already sit in. Once they are all lying correctly you can re-wind the loom end to ensure the threads are taut.

289

Continuous warp

It is always best to begin with a reel of thread to ensure you
don't run out before you finish setting up your loom.

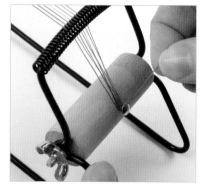

1 First work out how many threads you
will need. This needs to be the number
of beads across the width of your work
plus one. Tie the end of your thread
around a peg at one end of your loom.

2 Find the central groove in the coil at
the same end of your loom and then
count away from this half the number of
threads you will need. Lay your thread
into this first groove. Bring your thread
down to the other end of your loom and
lay it in the corresponding groove and
then take it around the peg at this end.

3 Take your thread back to the first end
with it lying in the next groove along
toward the central groove. Continue to
weave from one end to the other, filling
all the necessary grooves and taking
your thread around the pegs until you
have added one more thread than the
exact bead width of your piece.

290

Weaving on the loom

Once your loom is set up and ready to go,
the actual beading is very quick and
easy. Follow these simple steps.

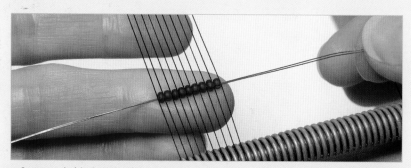

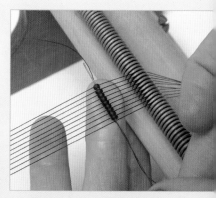

1 Cut a workable length of thread and
tie or tape this onto one of the rollers
at one end of your work. This is your
weaving, or weft, thread. Pick up all
the beads you need for your first row
onto your needle and slide them down
the thread.

2 If the piece you are beading is wider
than the length of your needle, pick
them up in batches instead. Bring your
thread up under the warp threads and
position the beads so that each one
sits into its own groove.

3 Use your finger underneath the beads
to push them upwards so that they sit
in their individual spaces and the bead
holes rise up to lie above the warp
threads. Take your needle and thread
so it comes around the top of the end
warp thread or threads and go back
through all of your beads so you end
up on the side you started. Check to
see if you have pierced any of your
threads by sliding the beads up and
down the warp threads and then bring
them back in line.

FIX IT

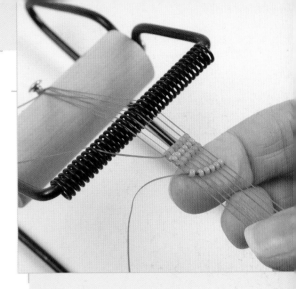

291 Piercing the thread

Piercing the thread means going through one of the warp threads with your weaving or weft thread. If you are planning on pulling the warp threads, you don't want to do this as it will mean you won't be able to pull all the threads and it can distort your work. In regular loom work it is not so disastrous but it can distort your work slightly. To reduce the risk:
• Use a blunt needle or thread the needle through the eye first.
• Push the beads up from the bottom and raise the holes—this gives your needle more space to go through the beads without accidentally piercing the warp threads.

If you have pierced your thread
If you discover just after adding a row that you have pierced your thread, undo your work by taking your needle off your thread and carefully removing all the beads in that row, then taking your thread back to the end of the previous row. This is especially important if you plan on using the pulled warps finishing method.

Checking for piercing
If you plan on finishing your work using the pulled warps method it is a good idea to check each row as you work it to ensure you haven't pierced any warp threads. Do this by sliding the beads in the last row up and down the warp threads and checking they can all move freely and no threads are caught or pierced.

292

Weaving a piece longer than your loom

Ensure when you set up the loom that you cut warp threads long enough for your piece and to weave in later. The excess thread can be rolled around the roller at the end of the loom nearest you when you start. As your work gets nearer to this end, loosen the tension on both rollers, gently roll them, and adjust your work away from you so you create more space to work in.

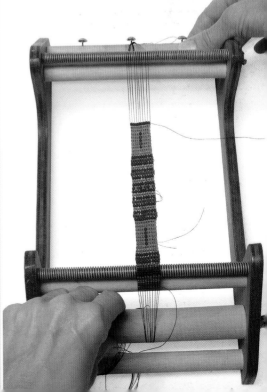

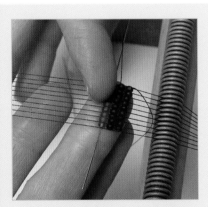

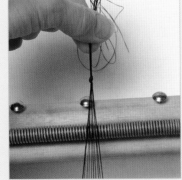

4 Continuing adding rows of beadwork, checking after each one for pierced threads, and adding new threads as you need them until your work is the length you require.

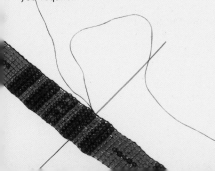

5 To take your work off the loom, loosen the end rollers to loosen the tension and lift your work off.

6 You now need to weave all of your weft or weaving thread ends into your work to secure them. As you do this make sure you don't pierce any threads if you plan on using the pulled warps method to finish.

293

Finishing your work

There are a number of different ways of finishing your work and this can often be the most difficult aspect of loom work. Read through all the different possibilities and decide which one works best for the project you have in mind, then turn to the relevant page number for more information.

Method	Pros	Cons
Leave the ends (see opposite)	• The easiest method, involves almost no work. • Ideal for hanging pieces for decoration.	• Not suitable to make finished jewelry. • May not suit all types of decorative work.
Plaiting the ends (see opposite)	• The second easiest method, involves very little work. • Looks neater than simply leaving the threads.	• Can be used for simple jewelry but the thread ends will have to be knotted together and unknotted each time it is worn. • May not suit all types of decorative work.
Backing your work (see opposite)	• Ideal for turning into finished jewelry. • Gives a more professional finish. • Tidies away and hides all the thread ends.	• You need to find a suitable clasp or way to turn it into wearable jewelry. • If you want to add a clasp, you can combine this method with weaving threads to the center to leave some warp threads to attach a finding to. • If it is a decorative piece, you may need to attach a suitable finding to hang it from. • Extra work when backing may not even be seen.
Pulled warps (see page 143)	• Hides all threads and gives a neat finish.	• No obvious way to attach a clasp to the work. • If it is a decorative piece you may need to attach a suitable finding to hang it from.
Weaving the threads to the center (see opposite)	• Leaves threads to attach findings to or hang work from.	• Extra work. • Bead holes can become full and trickier to get extra threads through.
Buttons, beads, and loops (see page 142)	• Ideal to turn your loom work into wearable jewelry. • Means you can color coordinate your fastening to your work without having to add any metal findings.	• Loops can be simply added to one end to hang up your work if it is decorative.
Integral buttonhole (see page 143)	• Means you can color coordinate your fastening to your work without having to add any metal findings.	• Trickier to bead. • Involves some planning ahead to include the buttonhole as you bead your loom work. • Only works with an odd number of beads across the width of your loom work.

294 Leave the ends

This is the simplest method of finishing your work and is ideal if you want to simply hang a piece of beadwork as decoration. Tie the thread ends into a knot and use this to hang your work.

295 Plaiting the ends

This is the second easiest way to finish your work and gives a neater look than simply leaving the ends. Separate your warp threads so you have three different bundles. Don't worry if these don't contain an even number of threads. Plait these together and then finish with a knot.

296 Backing your work

This is a convenient method of finishing your work as you don't need to deal with all of the warp threads. You can back your work with any fabric but a non-fray one such as felt, leather, suede, interfacing, or the right-sized ribbon is ideal.

1 Knot the ends of your warp threads together close to your work and place your beadwork onto your backing fabric with the threads lying between the work and the fabric.

2 Use a thread that matches the color of your backing or the beading and stitch the beadwork to the backing fabric. Secure the beadwork by threading under the end warp threads. If you want to hang your work, you can stitch a loop of thread, ribbon, or even a jump ring to the back from which it can hang. To turn your work into jewelry you can stitch a suitable clasp onto the backing or leave some warp threads that you weave into the center and use to attach a finding.

297 Weaving the threads to the center

This method is ideal if you want to turn your loom work into a piece of jewelry as you keep some threads that can be used to attach a clasp or calotte.

Weave as many of your individual warp threads as possible so they are exiting from the central point of your beadwork. This could be coming from either side of a central bead or between two central beads depending on whether there are an even or odd number of beads in the width of your work.

These threads can be knotted together and placed inside a calotte that can be attached to a clasp to finish.

298

Buttons, beads, and loops

This method uses beads or buttons at one end of your beadwork that thread through loops at the other end to secure your beadwork when worn. If your work is purely decorative, you can just add loops at one end to hang your work from.

1 Finish your loom work and then use two of your warp threads at one side to pick up two small beads and then a larger bead or button. Next pick up a turn bead and thread back through your button or large bead, the two small beads, and back into your work. Weave the thread into your work to secure and trim.

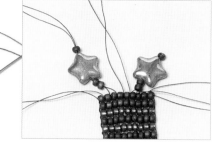

2 Repeat to use two other warp threads to attach more beads if required.

3 At the other end of your work, find the corresponding warp threads and use these to thread on two matching small beads.

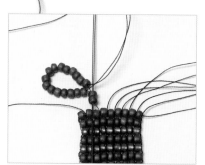

4 Use your threads to pick up enough beads to make a loop that will comfortably fit over your large beads or buttons, but not so large it will easily slip off.

5 Thread back into the body of your work and double check the loop fits your button or large bead. When you are happy with it, weave your threads into your work to secure and trim. Finish your work by weaving in any extra warp threads left. If your loom work is narrow you can just use one loop and bead or button to secure.

6 You can also use a different-shaped bead by exiting your work, picking up two or three small beads, and then separating your threads. Use each thread to enter your bead, one from each side, and then take each thread back into the smaller beads and back into your work.

299

Integral buttonhole

This method can be used with a bead or button at one end, as in the button, beads, and loop method, or with a larger bead or button sewn directly onto your beadwork at one end. You need to plan your work in advance and ensure you only use an odd number of beads across the width of your work. Also ensure you have selected your larger bead or button first so that you make the buttonhole the correct size.

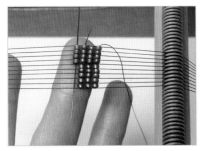

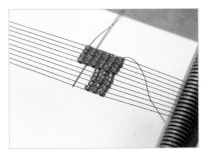

1 Begin your loom work and bead the first few rows. When you come to where you want to start your buttonhole, only pick up half the number of beads you need for the row, minus one. Thread back through those beads.

2 Continue adding short rows until you have added enough to create the size of the buttonhole you require. Weave back through these rows until you end up exiting the last full row at the other side of your work.

3 Begin to add corresponding short rows to form the other side of your buttonhole. Once you have beaded the size required, return to beading full rows until you have finished your loom work.

300

Pulled warps

This method gives you a quicker way to deal with your threads so you can end up with only two to tie in.

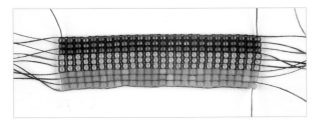

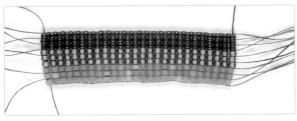

1 Bead your loom work, ensuring after every row that you haven't pierced any threads, and remove your work from your loom. Sticking tape over your loom work can help to keep the rows and work even and prevent it buckling up.

2 Starting at the bottom of your work, near the center, gently pull a warp thread so that it pulls all the way through from the top. Work slowly and gently because if you have pierced any threads, these will catch and distort your work.

3 Continue pulling warp threads until you reach the edge of your work, then return to the center and repeat for the remaining threads until you are left with just two ends to weave in and secure. If you do find you have pierced any threads, move onto the next warp thread and start again. It will simply mean you are left with more than two thread ends to finish.

301 Embellishing your work

Adding fringes and side embellishments will take your loom work from a flat, square piece of beadwork to one with more texture and shape.

SINGLE-BEAD EDGING
This adds a decorative yet simple look to your work. You can choose to use the same beads as in the main body of your piece or new ones to add contrast.

1 Finish your loom work as required and then, using a new thread, exit one of your edge beads. Pick up a new bead, thread under the edge warp thread, and then thread back down your new bead.

2 Continue adding single beads all along the length of your work.

TRIPLE-BEAD EDGING
Worked in a similar style to single-bead edging, this adds a picot of three beads along each edge.

1 Begin as for single-bead edging but instead pick up three beads. Thread under your warp thread and then back through the third bead picked up.

2 Pick up two beads, thread under the appropriate warp thread, and thread back down the second bead. Continue picking up two beads all the way along the edge of your work.

FIX IT

302 Loom work too short or narrow?

If you find your loom work piece too short or narrow you can always add extra beads and rows to it using square stitch.

---

303 Larger beads

If you want to use larger beads in your loom work, or a mix of bead width, you can place thread only in every other groove when setting up to give you more width between the warp thread.

---

304 Mixing beads

If you want to use a mix of bead widths, set up your loom with the warp threads wide enough apart to take your widest beads and then when you are adding narrower beads use more than one in each space.

SEE ALSO:

Working with
thread, page 88
Brick stitch,
page 96
Peyote stitch,
page 105
Square stitch,
page 110
Right-angle weave,
page 114
Loom work,
page 136

Moving on in beadweaving

Moving on in beadweaving takes you into adding fringes, loops, and other forms of embellishments. These are all great for adding texture and movement to a piece of beadwork. They can be short or long, even or random, identical or varied, all-over or confined to one place—the choice is yours. Once you understand what makes a fringe, loop, or embellishment and how to bead them from your work, you will be able to go on to explore and experiment with endless variations of your own.

305

Starting to fringe

A fringe is a length of beads hanging down from your work. They can be beaded in a endless variety of choices and can enhance your beadwork or become the main focus.

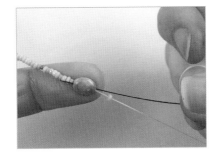

Missing the end bead of your strand, called the "turn bead," is what makes fringing work.

STIFF FRINGE

You may find that it is best to pull your fringes too tight when you bead them so they sit stiffly. This means that when the thread does stretch and loosen it will only do so an amount you are happy with and no more. Once you have finished your work you can run the fringes through your hands to loosen them and get movement back into them.

BEADING A FRINGE

The essential feature of a fringe is the turn bead. This is the bead (or set of beads) at the end of a fringe that stops all of your beads from falling off your thread. Missing out the turn bead on the return is what makes the fringe work. Bead a fringe by exiting your work, picking up the length of beads you want for the fringe plus the turn bead or beads. Miss the turn bead, or beads, and thread back up through all of the other fringe beads and back into your work.

PROTECT AGAINST SAGGING

Beading thread has a certain amount of stretch in it and with the weight of the beads used in your fringe it can stretch and loosen over time, with the result that a small amount of it can show at the top of your fringe. To stop this happening, always stretch your thread before you begin and pull your fringes tight when beading them.

306

Fringes from other stitches

Adding fringes to beadwork is a great way of adding more beads, color, movement, texture, and pattern. Exactly how you do it will depend on what stitch is used as your base.

BEADS WITH VERTICAL HOLES

These are stitches such as loom work or square stitch held sideways, as well as ladder, brick, and herringbone stitch.

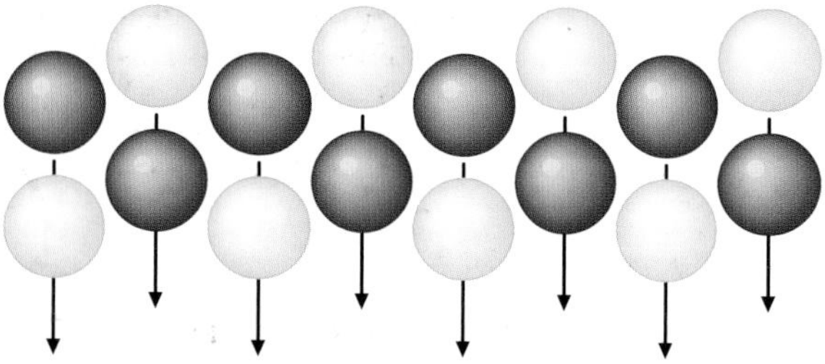

Here the bead hole runs up and down and it is easy to add fringes.

1 Begin by exiting one of the edge beads and picking up the necessary fringe and turn beads.

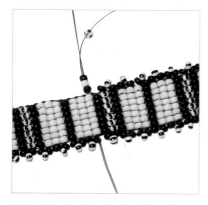

2 Miss the turn bead or beads and thread back through the rest of the fringe beads and into the main body of your work.

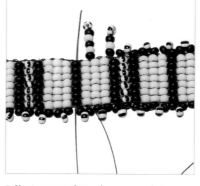

3 Next weave through your work to exit the next edge bead in the main body of your work and add another fringe. Repeat to add as many fringes as you require.

TRY IT

307   Mixing it up

You will find that some stitches fall into both categories. For example, on a piece of right-angle weave, some edge beads have a horizontal hole and some have a vertical hole—why not try adding a fringe to the two differently lying beads? On a piece of peyote stitch beadwork, the lowest-sitting beads have a horizontal hole, but so too do the beads in the row above and these can also have a fringe added to them—why not experiment with adding beads to both rows or just one? With square stitch and loom work, fringes can be added to the top and bottom rows, or along the edges, or both.

In right-angle weave, these edge beads have a horizontal hole, and are perfectly positioned for adding a decorative fringe.

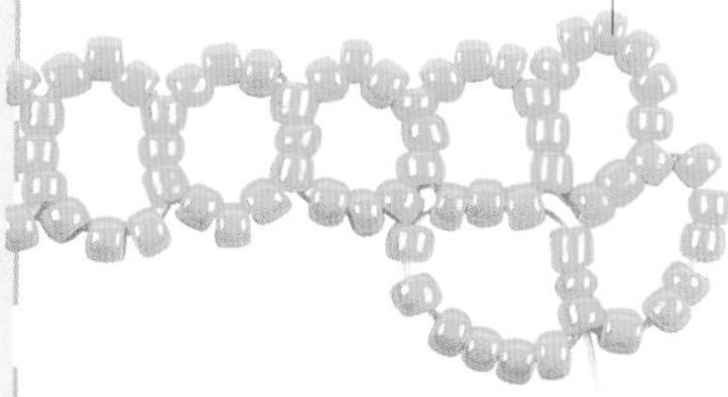

BEADS WITH HORIZONTAL HOLES

These are ladder, right-angle weave, and peyote stitch as well as the top and bottom rows of square stitch and loom work, or herringbone or brick stitch on their side. In these stitches the holes run from side to side and fringes need to be beaded slightly differently.

1 Exit the left-hand edge bead, making sure you are exiting the bead from the right-hand side. Pick up all your fringe beads plus your turn bead or beads.

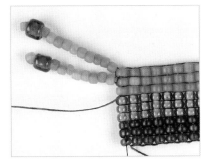

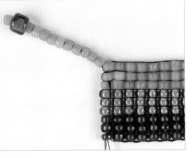

2 Miss the turn bead or beads and thread back up through all of your fringe beads and into the edge bead you were exiting, this time threading through from the left-hand side.

3 Weave through your work to exit the next edge bead and repeat, adding a fringe. Continue adding fringes until you have added as many as required.

308

Tightening your fringe

As you bead it is important to tighten each fringe to reduce the chances of sagging later. It can be tricky to do this but the main tip is to hold onto your turn bead or beads, while you pull your thread to tighten. This ensures the thread can move freely through your beads and pull up tight.

311

Loops

Loops are variations on fringes but don't have a turn bead at the end. Instead they are one continuous loop of beads which can be joined to the same bead it started from or to another bead.

Loops can exit and re-enter the same bead in the beadwork base.

For a variation on loops try taking your needle and thread back into a different bead in your beadwork base.

TRY IT

312 **Experiment with fringing**

Fringes don't all have to be the same length or use the same beads. Experiment with different patterns to create completely different looks.

This necklace (left) uses the same type of fringe with random amounts of seed beads picked up and a different large bead used as the turn.

Fringing with flower and leaf beads adds texture, color, and movement to the below bracelet.

The fringing on this lampshade keeps the same beads at the end of the fringe but different amounts of seed beads are used at the top to vary the lengths but keep the pattern going.

313

Embellishments

Embellishments are all those other beads, sequins, and charms sewn onto your work to further add a touch of color or texture. You can do this randomly or in a pattern, sparingly or all over—experiment to your heart's content.

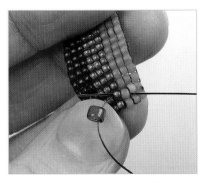

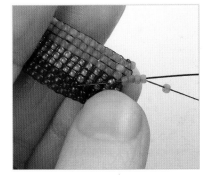

SINGLE-BEAD EMBELLISHMENTS
Simply exiting a bead in your work, picking up a bead, and then weaving back into your work will soon add surface decoration and embellishment.

SURFACE FRINGES
Think of these as short fringes added onto the surface of your work rather than hanging from an edge. They can be as small as one sequin and a turn bead, or longer to add more texture.

SURFACE LOOPS
Exiting one side of your beadwork, picking up a length of beads, and then threading into the other side of your bead will add loops that can either sit tight against your work, using fewer beads, or looser, using more beads.

TRY IT

314   **Fringing with no base beadwork**

Fringing can also be used to decorate jewelry and decorative items where there is no base beadwork. Why not make a strung necklace, attach a beading thread, and add fringing to it afterward?

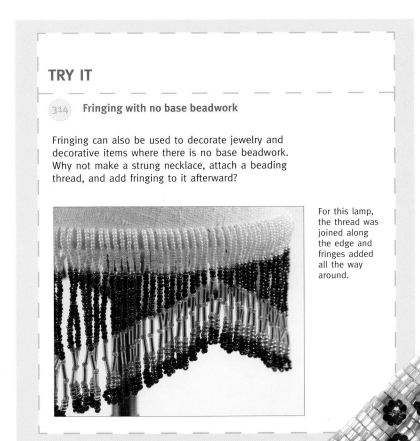

For this lamp, the thread was joined along the edge and fringes added all the way around.

These crystal flowers were sewn onto a base of square stitched hex beads.

Resources

Suppliers

Beadalon
440 Highland Blvd.,
Coatsville, PA 19320
www.beadalon.com

Beadbabe.com
14 Church St.,
PO Box 592, Vineyard Haven
MA 02568
www.beadbabe.com

Beadcats
PO Box 2840
Wilsonville, OR 97070-2840
(503) 625-2323
www.beadcats.com

Beadin' path, The
15 Main St.,
Freeport,
ME 04032
www.beadinpath.com

Blue Moon Beads
www.bluemoonbeads.com

Cartwright's Sequins & Vintage Buttons
11108 N. Hwy. 348
Mountainburg, AR 72946
(479) 369-2074
www.ccartwright.com

Charm Factory, Inc.
PO Box 91625,
Albuquerque, NM 87199-1625
866-867-5266
www.charmfactory.com

Fire Mountain Gems
One Fire Mountain Way
Grants Pass, OR 97526-2373
(800) 355-2137
www.firemountaingems.com

FusionBeads.com
(888) 781-3559

Lisa Peters Art
215 Demarest Ave., Closter
NJ 07624
(201) 784-0812
www.lisapetersart.com

Out on a Whim
121 E. Cotati Ave.
Cotati, CA 94931
(800) 232-3111
www.whimbeads.com

Shipwreck Beads
8560 Commerce Place Dr. NE,
Lacey, WA 98516
(800) 950-4232
www.shipwreckbeads.com

Stormcloud Trading Co.
www.beadstorm.com

Thunderbird Supply Company
www.thunderbirdsupply.com

Online resources

www.abeadstore.com
A selection of simple beading projects, tips, FAQs, and a retail area.

www.auntiesbeads.com
Online retailer with a wide range of beads and findings as well as resources for weekly projects and free video tutorials.

www.beadersshowcase.com
An online community with a place to showcase your work and chat to other members with groups catering to all types of beading who will offer challenging projects to stimulate your creativity.

www.beadingdaily.com
Site containing projects, information, contests, galleries, and chat.

www.beadingtimes.com
Excellent source of information on all aspects of jewelry design. Updated monthly.

www.beadmagazine.co.uk
Site with projects, galleries, and forums. Also features Bead TV, showing tutorials, workshops, and demonstrations.

http://beadwork.about.com/
An American site with an active forum and a lot of links and articles.

www.beadworkersguild.org.uk
A membership site publishing a journal and a selection of books, as well as running workshops and beading events.

www.crystalgems.co.uk
Information regarding crystal and gemstone properties and how they can be used with chakras and as remedies.

www.enijewelry.com
Amazing online tutorials on wire work; either pay to download the individual projects you require, or follow free links to beginners' lessons.

www.firemountain.com
An excellent online retailer with a huge range of gemstones and other supplies as well as a useful "encycloBEADia," gallery, and tutorials section.

www.jewelinfo4u.com
A vast source of information ranging from gemstone data to tools required for jewelry making and designer galleries.

www.merchantsoverseas.com
Information on all things Swarovski, with color, shape, and size charts, seasonal color trends, and an online retail area.

www.wire-sculpture.com
Excellent resource center on wire and metal skills, containing projects and ideas as well as information on pricing and marketing your work.

Magazines

Bead Magazine
www.beadmagazine.co.uk

Beadstyle
www.beadstylemag.com
Bi-monthly magazine with tutorials and supply lists incorporating a wide range of materials.

Bead and Button
www.beadandbutton.com
A magazine packed with loads of projects to challenge and inspire readers of all interests and abilities.

Societies

There are bead societies in most U.S. states—just contact your local library for details. Alternatively, a quick internet search will produce a list of possible societies and groups.

Austin Bead Society
P.O. Box 656
Austin, TX 78767-0656
Email: austinbeadsociety@yahoo.com
www.austinbeadsociety.org

Baltimore Bead Society
8510 High Ridge Road
Ellicott City, MD 21043
Email: baltbead@bcpl.net
www.baltobead.org

Bead Museum, The
5754 W Glenn Drive
Glendale, AZ 85301
www.thebeadmuseum.com

Bead Society of Greater Chicago
P.O. Box 8103
Wilmette, IL 60091-8103
www.bsgc.org

Bead Society of Greater New York, The
P.O. Box 6219
FDR Station
New York, NY 10150
Email: info@nybead.org
http://nybead.org

Bead Society of Greater Washington, The
The Jenifer Building, Ground Floor
400 Seventh Street Northwest
Washington, DC 20004
Email: info@beadmuseumdc.org
www.bsgw.org

Bead Society of New Hampshire, The
P.O. Box 356
Atkinson, NH 03811
Email: beadsocietynh@yahoo.com
www.nebeads.com/BSNH

Bead Society of Orange County, The
2002 N. Main Street
Santa Ana, CA 92706
www.beadsocietyoc.org
Upper Midwest Bead Society
3000 University Avenue SE, #5
Minneapolis, MN 55414

Cumberland Valley Bead Society
Box 41903
Nashville, TN 37204
Email: johnsoncaren@hotmail.com
www.cvbeads.net

Great Lakes Beadworkers Guild
P.O. Box 1639
Royal Oak, MI 48068-1639
www.greatlakesbeadworkersguild.org

International Society of Glass Beadmakers
1120 Chester Avenue #470
Cleveland, OH 44114
www.isgb.org

Los Angeles Bead Society, The
PO Box 241874
Culver City
CA 90024–9674

Madison Bead Society
P.O. Box 620383
Middleton, WI 53562-0383
Email: madisonbeadsoc@hotmail.com
www.madisonbeadsociety.org

National Bead Society
3855 Lawrenceville Hwy.
Lawrenceville, GA 30044
Email: ibs@beadshows.com
http://nationalbeadsociety.com

Northwest Bead Society
P.M.B. 564
4603 N.E. University Village
Seattle, WA 98105
www.nwbeadsociety.org

Oklahoma Bead Society
Teresa Davis, Librarian
5144 S New Haven Ave.
Tulsa, OK 74135
Email: teresadavis50@hotmail.com
www.okbeadsociety.com

Portland Bead Society
P.O. Box 997
Portland, OR 97207-0997
www.beadport.com

Rocky Mountain Bead Society (RMBS)
P.O. Box 480721
Denver, CO 80248-0721
Email: rmbs@rockybeads.org
www.rockybeads.org

San Antonio Bead and Ornament Society
Email: sabostx@hotmail.com
www.homestead.com/sabostx/

South Jersey Bead Society
53 Sunset Drive
Voorhees, NJ 08043-4941
Email: prancingpixel@yahoo.com
www.southjerseybeadsociety.org

Wyoming TumbleBeaders Bead Society
P.O. Box 1431
Cheyenne, WY 82003-1431
www.geocities.com/wyotumblebeaders/

Glossary

2-drop
When two or more beads are used at one time, but treated as though they were one bead.

Anneal
To slowly cool a glass bead in a kiln or annealing oven, to strengthen the interior of the bead.

Aught (or "o")
A unit of measurement for seed beads. Originally based on how many beads fit into 1in (2.5cm). Therefore, size 8 beads are bigger than size 15 beads.

AWG
American Wire Gauge. The measurement used to sell wire in the U.S.A.

Back through
To thread back through a bead in the opposite direction.

Bead reamer
Tool used to enlarge or smooth bead holes.

Bead release
A paste that is painted onto a mandrel to stop hot glass from sticking to it.

Bead soup
A mix of beads in different shapes, sizes, and colors.

Brick stitch
Beading stitch in which the rows sit flat beside each other but are offset, to resemble brickwork.

Bugle bead
Long, tubular seed bead.

Calottes
Small findings, also called clamshells, necklace tips, or necklace endings, used to hide unsightly knots in thread or to fasten the stringing material to the clasp.

Chain-nose pliers
Pliers with flat inner jaws that taper to a point. Also called snipe-nose pliers.

Circle through
To thread back through a bead in the same direction you originally went through it.

Cloisonné bead
Patterned bead made of filigree metal colored with enamel glazes.

Crimp beads
Small metal beads that, when squashed with crimping pliers, bite into the nylon surface of flexible beading wire to secure.

Crimping
The act of squashing crimp beads to secure them onto flexible beading wire.

Crimping pliers
Pliers with two specially designed notches used to squash crimp beads.

Culling
Removing beads if they are misshapen, odd colors, or the wrong size.

Decreasing
Removing beads or stitches to narrow your work.

Dominant hand
The hand you use most (i.e. your right hand if you are right-handed).

Eyepin
A length of wire with a loop at one end.

Findings
The small metal pieces used to finish jewelry, such as clasps, crimps, or earring hooks.

Flat circular
Beadwork performed flat but in a circular pattern.

Flat-nose pliers
Pliers with a flat inner jaw, the same width all the way along.

Flexible beading wire
A series of very fine strands of stainless steel coated in nylon, used to string jewelry and to finish with crimp beads. Also called beading or stringing wire, or beading cable.

Gauge (ga)
A term used to indicate the thickness of wire.

Gimp
Also called French wire, this is used to protect your thread from rubbing against metal findings.

Go through
To thread through a bead.

Headpin
A length of wire with a wider end that stops beads from falling off.

Herringbone stitch
Decorative stitch in which the beads are added in pairs and resemble a herringbone pattern.

Hex-cut bead
Bead with hexagonal sides.

Increasing
Adding extra beads or stitches to widen your work.

Jump ring
Small loop of metal that can be used to attach findings.

Ladder stitch
Basic beading stitch comprising of only one row of beads

Lampwork
A technique for making handmade glass beads using rods of glass heated in a flame and molded over a metal mandrel.

Mandrel
A metal rod used to form jump rings or glass beads.

Off-loom beadwork
Beadweaving stitches that are performed in the hands without a loom. This includes peyote and brick stitch as well as beaded chains and right-angle weave.

Overhand knot
A knot formed by making a loop in a piece of cord and pulling the end through it.

Picot
A 3-bead embellishment, usually applied along the edge or surface of your beadwork.

Peyote stitch
Decorative stitch that creates a "fabric" of beads by weaving them together by hand in an offset row method.

Rattail
Satin cord made for beading projects.

Right-angle weave
Also known as RAW, this is an off-loom stitch in which all the beads lie at right angles to each other.

Reef knot
Formed by tying a left-handed overhand knot and then a right-handed overhand knot, or vice versa. Also called a square knot.

Rosary pliers
Round-nose pliers with wire cutters in the handles specially designed to make rosary (or turned) loops.

Round-nose pliers
Pliers with rounded jaws that taper to a point.

Skip a bead
Missing a bead and threading through the next one.

Split ring
These are used to attach findings to your jewelry.

Square stitch
An off-loom beadweaving stitch that mimics the appearance of beadwork created on a loom. Each bead is connected by thread to each of the four beads surrounding it.

Step-up
To finish a row of beadwork and ensure you're in the correct position to bead the next row.

Stop bead
Also called a tension bead. A bead added to the start of your work to stop other beads from falling off the thread, and to help you maintain tension.

Tail-thread
The end of thread that you leave at the start and end of your work to use later to finish your beadwork.

Tension
How tight or loose your finished beadwork is.

Tubular
Beadwork worked around a three-dimensional tubular shape.

Turn bead
The end bead in a piece of fringing. This bead is skipped when you thread back through the fringe.

Turned loop
A small loop at the end of a wire. Also known as a rosary loop.

Wrapped loop
A decorative and secure method of creating a loop on wire.

Zipping up
When the edges of a piece of flat beadwork are joined to make it tubular.

Index

Fold-out flap

Essential measurements

Fold out this flap to find an at-a-glance table of common bead sizes and a chart explaining AWG (American Wire Gauge). Keep the flap open as you work through the techniques in this book for easy-reference to this essential information.

Credits

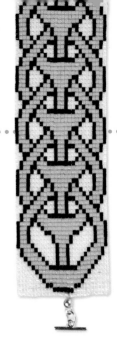

Quarto would like to thank the following agency for kindly supplying images for inclusion in this book:

• Shutterstock

All finished jewelry is the work of Jean Power, who can be contacted at jean@jeanpower.com, with the exception of the design that appears on page 2 (top) and page 15 (bottom), which is the work of Sorrel Wood (CupboardOfGood.etsy.com).

With thanks to Moira Clinch, for the loan of her necklace for photography (page 15, top).

All other images are the copyright of Quarto Publishing plc. While every effort has been made to credit contributors, Quarto would like to apologize should there have been any omissions or errors—and would be pleased to make the appropriate correction for future editions of the book.